D1607873

Southern Literary Studies

Fred Hobson, Editor

Published by Louisiana State University Press
Manufactured in the United States of America
First printing

Designer: Barbara Neely Bourgoyne
Typeface: Avenir, display; Chaparral Pro, text
Printer and binder: Edwards Brothers, Inc.

Library of Congress Cataloging-in-Publication Data

Weaks-Baxter, Mary.
   Reclaiming the American farmer : the reinvention of a regional
mythology in twentieth-century southern writing / Mary Weaks-Baxter.
      p. cm. — (Southern literary studies)
   Includes bibliographical references and index.
   ISBN 0-8071-3129-6 (alk. paper)
  1. American literature—Southern States—History and criticism.
2. American literature—20th century—History and criticism.
3. Pastoral fiction, American—History and criticism.
4. Southern States—Intellectual life—1865– 5. Southern States—
In literature. 6. Regionalism in literature. 7. Farm life in literature.
8. Farmers in literature. 9. Myth in literature. I. Title. II. Series.
PS261.W43 2006
810.9'3263—dc22

                                        2005020318

The paper in this book meets the guidelines for permanence and durability
of the Committee on Production Guidelines for Book Longevity of the
Council on Library Resources. ⊗

Reclaiming the American Farmer

THE REINVENTION OF A REGIONAL MYTHOLOGY IN

TWENTIETH-CENTURY SOUTHERN WRITING

MARY WEAKS-BAXTER

LOUISIANA STATE UNIVERSITY PRESS   BATON ROUGE

In memory of Floyd C. Watkins

and for my parents,
Thomas Elton and Elizabeth Wright Weaks

Contents

Acknowledgments

This book finds its roots in the very soil of my parents' Tennessee farmland. Without my parents' strong affection for their southern roots and their insistence that my sister and I know the family home places and burying grounds, I never would have had the sense of a regional past that led me to choose the field of southern literature as the focus of my life's work. This book is thus dedicated to my parents, Thomas Elton and Elizabeth Wright Weaks, and to Floyd C. Watkins, my teacher and friend, who passed away in May 2000. In a course on Faulkner, during my freshman year at Emory University, Floyd first showed me both the pleasures and the challenges of studying southern literature. Floyd was a teacher and scholar who was truly passionate about his work. In the last few years of his life, he read an early version of this book and encouraged me to think more about ways to focus my argument and to write with a voice that was truly my own. Without his guidance, this book would not exist.

This book has evolved over a number of years. In the late 1980s, I completed a dissertation on Allen Tate, Caroline Gordon, and Robert Penn Warren that evolved into chapter 2. I thank Albert Devlin, my dissertation advisor at the University of Missouri–Columbia, for his comments and support in that earliest stage.

An important part of my research has been my visits to the South from my home in northern Illinois. Thanks to Linda Garner for acting as my guide to Oxford, Mississippi, and for her comradeship at many an academic meeting. Melba Smith spent many days with me exploring Warren country on the Tennessee-Kentucky border, and my aunt, Elnor McMahan Corgan, opened her Kentucky home to me so that I might spend time over a summer break for researching southern writers with connections to her area.

Since I first came to Rockford College in 1988, a number of my present and former colleagues have encouraged me in my work by writing in support of my applications for various Rockford College grants. In that regard, I would especially like to thank John Glass, Joel Tibbetts, Tim O'Hare, and Susan Johnston. My colleague and friend Christine Bruun has always been supportive and ever encouraging when my work has become frustrating, and Wesley Berry and John Glass both made invaluable suggestions concerning revisions and talked with me often about my progress. I am especially indebted to the Faculty Development Committee of Rockford College for their support in the way of released time, travel to libraries, a sabbatical, and research assistance, and to the Hazel Koch fund of Rockford College for research support.

At Rockford College, I have also been most fortunate to have the assistance of Marianne Musso for help with preparing the manuscript copy. Samantha Guarino spent many hours checking the accuracy of quotations and collecting research materials. Her work has been superb. Over the years, I have taught a number of courses in southern literature at Rockford College, and I am grateful to my many students who were willing to engage in lively discussions and to share with me their northern and midwestern perspectives on southern writers.

Because of my need to order many items through inter-library loan, I owe a special debt of gratitude to Audrey Wilson, of the Howard Colman Library of Rockford College, who processed my many requests. The staff in the special collections departments at Vanderbilt, Yale, and Princeton Universities also helped tremendously with my requests for materials.

When I completed a solid draft of the manuscript, Fred Hobson was very gracious in agreeing to read it. For his careful reading and encouragement, I am especially grateful. Candis LaPrade and John Easterly have made my work with Louisiana State University Press a pleasure, and I am quite honored to be numbered among the Press's authors.

A special thanks goes to Carolyn Perry, my friend and co-editor on two books on southern women writers, who has taught me so much about writing and who is the type of woman I aspire to be. Carolyn has always been more than willing to read multiple versions of manuscripts I have sent to her, even when she has been overloaded with work of her own.

In the end, it is to my family that I owe the greatest debt. Although my husband, Brent Baxter, came to cringe every time I mentioned the word "yeoman," without him, I would never have completed this book. Brent and our son, Andrew, have brought a comfort and happiness to my life that has renewed my passion for literature and for writing. My hope for Andy, who has been lulled to sleep many a night by the sound of my typing in the study next to his room, is that he, too, will have the great fortune to discover his life's passion. Both Brent and Andy keep me grounded and ever mindful of the importance of living fully.

Reclaiming the American Farmer

Introduction

When visitors first approach the Hermitage, Andrew Jackson's home in Nashville, what they first see is a white-pillared plantation house in the Greek Revival style. A side view of the front porch, however, shows the deception of the house's façade. First built with a comparatively plain façade in the Federal style, with only a fanlight and sidelights ornamenting the entry, the Hermitage was reconstructed by Jackson so that the front of the house, complete with six white columns, gives the appearance of being bolder than it is. A new façade was literally slapped on to give the impression that the house had always been in the latest fashion.

Something of this remaking, remodeling, and reinventing has always been at work in the South, and in discussions of the South and its history. Even in as unlikely a place as northern Illinois, where I now live, scholars associated with a nearby think tank called the Rockford Institute continue to promote a view of southern history that attempts to portray the Southern cause during the Civil War not as a fight over slavery but instead as a struggle against centralized government. Less than a two-hour drive from U. S. Grant's home in Galena, Illinois, and within shooting distance of the Wisconsin border, the institute is the home base for scholars who very publicly endorse thinking that is in line with organizations such as the League of the South. Promoting a neo-Confederate view, the league promotes a benign view of southern history, one that does not see the South's past as tightly bound with issues of race.

Such façade-building should not be a surprise to a reader of southern literature. Nevertheless, scholars of southern literature tend to overlook the rather dramatic attempts at dismantling façades—conservative or otherwise—during the Southern Literary Renaissance of 1900 to 1960. Although scholars traditionally have referred almost without fail to World War I as an impetus for the renaissance, Carol Manning makes a sound case for dating its beginnings to the turn of the century. Explaining that many women at the turn of the century were becoming increasingly dissatisfied with the traditional values that framed southern womanhood, Manning argues that modern southern literature developed as women writers began to examine and question women's place in southern society (244). The ending date of 1960 takes into account the great influence the civil rights movement had on the transition from southern modernism into what many have called a second southern literary renaissance. The following pages focus specifically on literary works of the first Southern Renaissance, but the conclusion looks to the second to examine the literary inheritance of writers of the contemporary South.

The first Southern Renaissance was not only a period of literary proliferation in the southern states but also a coming of age of the region's literature. It was a rethinking of those earlier façades that had emphasized the South as planter society. It was also a time of façade-building, as a wide-ranging group of southern writers reconstructed southern history based on a variety of political and literary motivations. If, in fact, the Southern Renaissance saw cohesiveness among writers of different races, genders, and economic levels, these new façades were focused more specifically on southern democratic ideals that were largely valued in Thomas Jefferson's notion of the American farmer.

The sense of urgency some writers felt about the need to reshape, revise, and rename the southern house—that is, the South itself—is quite clear in the words of W. J. Cash, who framed what has been called the definitive portrait of the southern plain folk in *The Mind of the South* (1941). Cash explains that in order to understand the true South, readers must recognize that the Old South was not the mythologized world of the southern planter but rather the world of the yeoman farmer. The only aristocracy in the antebellum South, according to Cash, was limited to "a narrow world" in Virginia where tobacco, rice, and indigo could be raised on a large scale. Cash claims that popular culture of his time continued to identify antebellum whites who were not planters as "white-trash," and although "nobody any longer holds to the Cavalier thesis in its overt form, it remains true that the popular mind still clings to it in essence" (4). Cash describes the legend of the Old South as a "sort of stage piece out of the eighteenth century, wherein gesturing gentlemen move soft-spokenly against a background of rose gardens and dueling grounds, through always gallant deeds" (ix). Arguing that the South is "no product of Cloud-Cuckoo-Town," he writes that it actually "proceeds from the common American heritage, and many of its elements are readily recognizable as being simply variations on the primary American theme" (viii).

Cash's South is a world with decidedly American ties, grounded in a tradition associated with the frontier and individualism. Cash explains how efforts in the 1940s to improve the region's farm structure depended, in large part, on safeguarding and extending the class of yeoman farmers (425). Throughout the book, Cash highlights the yeoman's role in the southern past and present as a key to a successful future for the region, and although he concludes that he will "venture no definite prophecies . . . in face of the forces sweeping over the world in the fateful year of 1940" (429), it is clear that he ties the region's promise to the history and culture of its plain folk, not its planters.

Cash urges readers to look at the South as one might look at "one of those churches one sees in England." The church's "façade and towers, the windows and clerestory, all the exterior and superstructure are late Gothic of one sort of another," but by looking into the nave, the aisles, and choir, "you find the old mighty Norman arches of the twelfth century. And if you look into its crypt, you may even find stones cut by Saxon, brick made by Roman hands" (x). Cash's English church is, in fact, like Andrew Jackson's Hermitage, hiding its character behind white columns. In order to discover the sustaining roots of the South, one must look past the façade to its interior. Cash explains that his book represents such an effort. Nevertheless, *The Mind of the South* has been criticized for largely ignoring the intellectual and literary life of colonial Virginia and for taking little account of the roles of African Americans and women in the South. Yet because Cash focused his book specifically on white males in his own piedmont South, his book exemplifies one southerner's intense desire to set the record straight, to reframe the South in a history that he believed provided essential truths about his homeland.

The first Southern Renaissance was a movement among southern writers like Cash to find a usable past for the South, one that provided a new myth that could keep southern culture and literature alive, promote southern ideologies beyond the region's borders, and sell southern literature to northern publishers. The new myth that came to the forefront focused not on the plantation culture that shaped nineteenth-century southern literature but instead on the folk, the common people who farmed the earth and who were rooted in the values of Jeffersonian agrarianism and democracy. While many southern writers continued to view the plantation as the defining element of southern life, others came down squarely on the side of the yeoman farmer. In reframing southern literature, and thus southern history, within the context of the common man and woman, southern writers recovered a usable past, a viable myth that offered promise of renewal and purpose.

In *The Ethnic Southerners*, George Tindall asks, "Is there not yet something more than nostalgia to the idea of the South? Is there not some living heritage with which the modern southerner can identify? Is there not, in short, a viable myth of the South?" (39). But what constitutes a usable past or a viable myth? Both in and out of the South in the years between 1900 and 1960, the message of the Lost Cause still lingered. The nineteenth-century South and its literature were clearly shaped by the myth of the planter ruling over a happy plantation, a myth that was used to gain support for slavery before the Civil War and for white supremacy afterward. Whereas the ultimate failure of the Old South and of the cavalier in the years of civil war provided a powerful myth of the past for many twentieth-century white southerners, this past was not a particularly viable or usable one because it emphasized failure, defeat, death, and the end of a culture. And it certainly was not a viable or usable past for black southerners. By the turn of the century, many southern writers began consciously searching to create new myths for the South and to reframe southern history and culture. Their attempts suggest their desire to explain how the South fit in with the rest of the United States—and, in some cases, to show how the South was superior to the rest of the nation. The literature of the period also focuses on finding a place for the South within an American framework that oftentimes marginalized the southern population. This new framework revised southern history in an essentially American context.

Southern writers portrayed the common folk for a variety of reasons, yet all in all, these writers achieved similar goals. Some, like the Nashville Agrarians, banded together to promote a southern way of life (i.e., the value of agrarian communities) as opposed to a northern one. Taking a decidedly conservative view of southern politics, the Agrarians were in line with a tradition of southern intellectuals who believed that the perpetuation of individual property rights and the role of the farmer were vital to southern conservative political thought. At the same time, marginalized southerners such as women, African Americans, and Appalachians saw opportunities for reconsidering and rebuilding their own lives within southern society. Ellen Glasgow, for example, used the figure of the common folk—in particular, the southern pioneer—to re-create the role of woman in southern society. Glasgow shared with other women writers of the Southern Renaissance, such as Olive Dargan and Zora Neale Hurston, an awareness of the mystical and mythical relationship between woman and the earth. Others, like Jean Toomer, suggested that the southern black should take from the southern earth not a continuing history of social deprivation but a folk culture of power and strength. For the farmer/poet Jesse Stuart, the southern Appalachian Mountains inspired a body of literature that he would cultivate and nourish like a crop he might till from the southern soil.

In the twentieth century, industrialization was crushing the southern rural way of life, not the Civil War, and southern writers wrote in reaction. Their work thus twines the modernist sense of loss and the struggle for renewal and hope. By embracing the American "myth of migration," southern characters like Elizabeth Madox Roberts's Ellen Chesser and Harriette Arnow's Gertie Nevels ultimately find they contain that potential for renewal and hope. In reframing southern literature, and therefore southern history, within the context of the common man and woman, writers were able to recover a usable past, a viable myth that offered promise of renewal and purpose and that helped them to find a place for themselves and for the South in the world at large.

In the figure of the common man and woman, or the southern "folk," writers wove together the various threads of southern literature. Even though writers are grouped under the name "southern" in anthologies and critical studies, southern literature is actually quite fragmented, divided along lines of gender, race, economics, and region. Perhaps those lines are even more distinct in southern literature because they are the same divisions that helped to create southern slave culture. Defining what makes literature "southern" has been difficult for scholars. In the past, for example, women, African American, and southern Appalachian writers have often been relegated to the peripheries of southern literature. Not until recent years, for instance, has the Harlem Renaissance been discussed in relation to the South, even though some of the leading figures of that movement were southern. Because of his race, Toomer would not have been viewed as part of the Southern Renaissance when it was happening. Writers of southern Appalachia have also had a tentative place in the canon. Yet what unifies the literature of the Southern Renaissance—whether written by women or men, white or black, prosperous or poor—are the southern folk. Although the plantation South continued to play a prominent role, the common man and woman shaped the literature of the renaissance.

In his foreword to *Brother to Dragons: A New Version,* Robert Penn Warren writes, "Historical sense and poetic sense should not, in the end, be contradictory, for if poetry is the little myth we make, history is the big myth we live, and in our living, constantly remake" (xiii). Likewise, Michael Kreyling, a contemporary scholar, explains in his *Inventing Southern Literature,* "It is not so much southern lit-

erature that changes in collision with history but history that is sub-
tly changed in collision with southern literature" (ix). Southerners
have long been attempting to re-create themselves and their region
through literature. In the twentieth century, the figure of the southern folk offered the possibilities of renewal and of a new order, of
celebrating an agrarian southernness. Writers in the modern period
desired to re-envision the South, and the folk offered a new vision.
The farmer pitted a southern way of life against northern industrialization, but the farming or yeoman tradition in the South was also
rooted in Jeffersonian idealism—an American ideal with southern
roots. For some writers of the modern period, reinterpreting southern history through the figure of the Jeffersonian farmer represented
an opportunity to point out that marginalized persons are as much
a part of the American democracy and of southern society as are
white males. For other writers, embracing the ideal of the yeoman
was a way for the South to reengage with the rest of the United States
during World War I and in the years following. For still others, the
yeoman ideal symbolized a new struggle against northern aggres-
sion and promoted a South that appeared to be more realistic and
pertinent than did the plantation South of the nineteenth century.

A number of writers of the modern South reaffirmed and preserved southern agrarian communities in their literature by confirm-
ing the essential Americanness of southern literature and the essential
southernness of American history. There are variations among the
American figures in the literary works I have chosen to cover in this
book. Some are pioneers, others are yeoman farmers, while others till
someone else's soil. At their root, they are all figures who have gained
independence—or are searching to gain independence—as tillers of
the earth. They are figures modeled after the Jeffersonian ideal of the
democratic American who gains individual strength, sustenance, and
social and political power through a relationship with the soil.

Clearly, this shift in southern literature was in part influenced by
the economic situation of the times. The common man and woman
held promise in suggesting how the United States might survive the
years of depression following the stock market crash of 1929. Outsiders viewed the South as a backward region because it was primarily a

rural economy. The southern farmers might find their greatest threat in the modern world of industrialization, as the cavalier found his defeat in the years of civil war. But, ironically, the yeoman's salvation could perhaps be seen in the Great Depression. Some supported returning to subsistence farming as the way to relieve the poverty of the depression years. Through characteristic ingenuity and practicality, and taking responsibility for self and family, the yeoman could be the salvation for America.

The agrarian model of the yeoman farmer is firmly bound within an American tradition, and it competed with the myth of the planter in the first several decades of the nineteenth century. Although the antebellum and postbellum Souths were inextricably tied to plantation mythology, that was not the case in the early years of the United States and in the first few decades of the nineteenth century. While writers such as Hector St. Jean de Crèvecoeur helped to define America as an agricultural nation, it was southerner Thomas Jefferson who solidified the new country's prospects in agrarianism. Jefferson's yeoman farmer was the model of independence, living on a small farm, raising crops for the family, surviving close to the earth, and developing a personal relation to the soil. Jefferson's often-quoted lines seem forever ingrained in the American consciousness: "Those who labor in the earth are the chosen people of God, if ever He had a chosen people . . . Corruption of morals in the mass of cultivators is a phenomenon of which no age nor nation has furnished an example" (280). The agrarian model had specific implications for the government that Jefferson envisioned. The farmer would be the foundation upon which the new country was built: the small landowners were to be "the most precious part of a state" (280). Their ability to sustain themselves economically and the moral values they accumulated through their relationship with the earth made them model citizens. In Jefferson's view and in the views of other of the founding fathers, the yeoman was not only the inheritor of a tradition that associated the pastoral with a utopia, or the Garden of the New World, but also a symbol of the republic itself. The farmer was associated with patriotism, with the individual struggle and support of American democracy.

Despite the idealism in which he held the American farmer, Jefferson's own life suggested a growing tension between the model of the yeoman and the cavalier planter. Jefferson might have written of the yeoman as the promising figure of a new country, but in reality his life reflected a conflict. He owned numerous slaves, whom he never freed even at his death. He wrote of the values of the sustenance farm, but he owned thousands of acres of land. He was the cavalier planter.

Nevertheless, in spite of Jefferson's inconsistencies, the yeoman ideal remained so powerful a myth that southerner Andrew Jackson was helped to the presidency of the United States by his claim to it. "Old Hickory" gained his reputation in the Battle of New Orleans where, as one Georgia congressman proclaimed, the "American Husbandman, fresh from his plough," reigned victorious over the British enemy. Jackson's "hardy free born race" of men were immortalized in the words of a song entitled "The Hunters of Kentucky" that was said to have been so popular that it could be heard sung or whistled most any day on the streets of American cities. The catchy tune helped increase Jackson's popularity among the American people, but Jackson, who served as president from 1829 to 1837, stood forth, more importantly and more fundamentally, as the symbol of his age. He was the image of Democratic America, the plain man. All the same, like Jefferson's life at Monticello, the reality of Jackson's life at the Hermitage in Nashville was closer to the cavalier ideal. Although Jackson called his Tennessee land his "farm," it was actually a plantation. Jackson's contemporary critics even chastised him for this disparity; one said, "The comparison of the occupation of our hardy yeomanry to that of a man whose plantation is worked by slaves and superintended by an overseer is almost too ridiculous to be seriously noticed" (Watson 17). Although the reality was that Jackson was a planter, he claimed to be the yeoman. American voters believed, too, in Jackson as representative of the yeomanry, and he gained political power because that mythology was recognized as American. Jacksonian Democrats were not soundly defeated by their Whig opponents until the Whigs developed what they called their "log cabin and hard cider" campaign.

In the years following Jackson's presidency, as sectional divisions widened, the South increasingly associated itself with the planter and the plantation. This ideal helped support slavery and isolate the South from the rest of the United States. The year 1832 actually marks a turning point in the South. Six years after the death of Thomas Jefferson, it saw the publication of the first major plantation novel, John Pendleton Kennedy's *Swallow Barn*. That year, the members of the Virginia legislature were also debating the future of their state. Charles J. Faulkner, a delegate from Berkeley County in the Shenandoah Valley, called for the abolition of slavery in the state. Faulkner believed that the plantation was driving the small farm into oblivion. While he referred to what he called "the slothful and degraded African," he described the white farmer in the most idealistic of terms: "Our native, substantial, independent yeomanry, constitute our pride, efficiency and strength; they are our defence in war, our ornaments in peace; and no population, I will venture to affirm, upon the face of the globe, is more distinguished for an elevated love of freedom—for morality, virtue, frugality and independence, than the Virginia peasantry west of the Blue Ridge" (Smith 152). According to Faulkner, Virginia had a choice to make—between the plantation slave system and Jefferson's farmer. Faulkner uses the term "peasantry" not in a derogatory manner but as a reflection of the hard work and endurance that he valued. Hard work elevated an individual, according to Faulkner.

Despite Faulkner's persistence, other southerners increasingly associated agricultural labor with what George Fitzhugh of Virginia described as "the most arduous, least respectable, and worst paid of all labor" (Smith 164). The slave system conveniently filled that gap. In effect, Virginia chose the mythology of the planter. By the 1850s, Frederick Law Olmsted, a northern journalist who traveled extensively in the South and wrote about the region, portrayed southern farmers as a class of southern rural whites who are "very much more incapable of being improved and elevated, than the most degraded peons of Mexico" (506). Increasingly, the South came to be represented as a section with highly drawn socioeconomic lines, with southerners typically categorized as planter, poor white, or black slave. Even history seems to suggest that the plantation reigned in the antebellum

South, although the number of farmers actually far outnumbered planters. Indeed, myth seems to have outweighed reality when the Old South was concerned.

By the time of the Civil War, the cavalier and his plantation were firmly secured as the mythology at the focus of southern society and culture. John Esten Cooke captured the strength of the cavalier myth in the South when he wrote in 1863 of the war as "the bludgeon against the rapier—the crop-eared Puritan against the Cavalier." Likewise, a Tennessee lieutenant is said to have marched off to war certain that the North could not win against a South framed in a tradition of chivalry and honor. "The scum of the North *cannot* face the chivalric spirit of the South," he firmly believed (Jimerson 127). Many white yeoman farmers marched off to war believing that plantation culture modeled values that they themselves saw as central to their own aspirations as farmers. Planter mythology also held that such a system could control the African American population of the South. Whatever their reasons, many white farmers fought the war for a southern way of life that was not their own. The stories are not typically told of the high number of southern troops who actually deserted the army, preferring to return home to their farms and their families rather than fight for a cause that seemed lost to many of them even before Appomattox Courthouse.

In a fascinating study entitled *Yeoman versus Cavalier: The Old Southwest's Fictional Road to Rebellion* (1993), literary scholar Ritchie Devon Watson, Jr., examines the South's antebellum divergence from the myth of the yeoman farmer to a reliance on the myth of the cavalier to support slavery and the Lost Cause. Historians like Charles S. Sydnor and Henry Nash Smith confirm in their studies of the antebellum South this shift from the agrarian to the planter myth. Yet while Ritchie Watson focuses specifically on what he refers to as the enshrinement of the planter myth, I propose that American models of the common man and woman—the yeoman farmer, the pioneer farmer— reared their heads again in the literature of the twentieth-century South and became a driving force in the literature of the century.

Such a turning point finds its roots in the postbellum years. When, for example, southern poet Sidney Lanier wrote in 1880 that "the New South means small farming," he was helping to create a new myth for the South. The "quiet rise of the small farmer," according to Lanier, meant a new era of stability: "Small farming means, in short, meat and bread for which there are no notes in bank; pigs fed with home-made corn . . . yarn spun, stockings knit, butter made and sold (instead of bought); eggs, chickens . . . products of natural animal growth, and grass at nothing a ton." With his statement Lanier rightly refers to the legacy of a civil war that broke apart large plantations into smaller farms and to the South's obvious need to move beyond the devastation of war and Reconstruction. But noted historian C. Vann Woodward also points out that although Lanier and others were quite taken with this new democratic model for the South, it was not the reality of life in the region. Lanier's vision might have been an "inspired" one, according to Woodward, but "it represented everything that the Southern farmer was *not* and *had not*." During the years of Reconstruction, the southern plantation system of slavery had been replaced by a tenant system of poverty, but Lanier and many others saw the yeoman farmer as "breaking up the plantation system" and the Civil War as the instrument that brought "economic democracy" to the South (175). Despite the fact that (or perhaps because) the yeoman myth was not the reality, it persisted.

By the postbellum years, the South was in the straits of poverty and destitution, and men like Lanier saw the small farmer as a figure that might help cultivate sectional reunion. Although the South faced serious poverty in the postbellum years and in the early decades of the twentieth century, by the 1920s the cavalier planter became increasingly associated with the decline of the South and the farmer with its rise. American society was built on agrarian values as most any history book will attest, or at least that is the myth that has been used to define American society and thus to represent the roots of American democracy. The yeoman was a figure who at once tied the southerner to his agrarian roots and defined southern society as a vital model of what American society would need to be if it were to survive in the modern world. Indeed, a new myth had been formed for the South—one that seemed more usable, more durable, and in many ways more practical.

Perhaps one of the most pointed examples of the creation of this new myth of the yeoman farmer is within the work of historian Frank Owsley, one of the Agrarian writers included in *I'll Take My Stand* and a noted southern historian who spent his career at Vanderbilt University. Owsley believed that the history books needed correcting because they had long portrayed the South as a region of large plantations. Instead, he argued, the South was actually composed of small farms farmed by the common folk. Owsley writes in his 1949 *Plain Folk in the Old South,* in an introduction notably entitled "Southern Society: A Reinterpretation," that during the later years of the antebellum period, those travelers and critics of the South who wrote about the region generally identified two groups of whites: slaveholders and "poor whites." "Moreover, whether or not they intended to do so, they created the impression in the popular mind that the slaveholder was a great planter living in a white-columned mansion, attended by a squad of Negro slaves who obsequiously attended his every want and whim . . . They crowded everyone not possessed of considerable wealth off the good lands and even the lands from which modest profits might be realized; they dominated politics, religion, and all phases of public life" (1). The rest of the white population (with a few exceptions, Owsley notes) was identified as "poor whites" or "poor white trash" and they were "a sorry lot indeed" (1). "They were illiterate, shiftless, irresponsible, frequently vicious, and nearly always addicted to the use of 'rot gut' whiskey and to dirt eating" (2), "the first version of *Tobacco Road,*" Owsley says (5). This was not the reality of antebellum southern society, Owsley argues, for the antebellum population of the South was actually composed primarily of small farmers—not plantation owners or "poor white trash." In effect, Owsley attempts to revise southern history, to reinterpret the region as a much more democratic place, and thus freer from the taint of plantation slavery.

Such a distinct shift of influence has had clear implications for southern literature following the first Southern Literary Renaissance. Although the majority of the chapters in this book examine the ways in which writers of the renaissance reframed southern literature within an American context of Jeffersonian agrarianism, I also include a chapter on Faulkner and on the readings of two Faulkner scholars who were clearly influenced by their own desires to reframe southern history. Writing during the civil rights movement, for example, M. E. Bradford reinterpreted Faulkner's Yoknapatawpha writings within a context that represented the yeoman farmer as the ideal at the center of Faulkner's work—despite the fact that Faulkner's yeomen play minor roles. Elizabeth Fox-Genovese and Eugene D. Genovese argue convincingly in "M. E. Bradford's Historical Vision" that although the burden of slavery is a thread that runs through Faulkner's work, Bradford, a prominent Faulkner scholar, "knew as much, but, like many of Faulkner's protagonists, he did not always want to know . . . he effectively excised the memory of slavery from the South he sought to claim and preserve" (91). In effect, Bradford deemphasizes the tragic nature of Faulkner's work and reframes it within the context of the yeoman farmer rather than the planter, suggesting that Faulkner's world was a much more democratic one than is generally recognized by readers.

The influence of the yeoman myth also has clear implications for contemporary southern writing, as the last chapter of my book attests. Southern history and literature have long been shaped by the boundaries imposed by society that limit individuals by race, gender, economics, and region. What becomes increasingly apparent about contemporary southern literature, however, is that southern voices from all walks of life are now speaking up—and have the power to do so. Contemporary southern literature is also much more a literature of healing and reconnection than was the literature of the modern South, and reformulating individual relationships with the southern soil is at the heart of this attempt. Contemporary southern literature is not a literature of defeat—thanks to the legacy left by modern writers who believed the future of southern literature lay not in a return to the myth of the planter but in the re-creation of an even older myth founded in the American ideals of Jeffersonian democracy.

In re-visioning the South's past within an American framework, southern writers were actually attempting to find what Van Wyck Brooks in 1918 termed as a "usable past." When Brooks wrote in an essay printed in *Dial* of "creating a usable past" for the United States, he set forth a goal that I believe became the essential focus of a number of writers of the first southern literary renaissance. Whether they had read Brooks's essay or not, these writers were at heart searching for a usable past for the South. Such a usable past tapped into not only the notion of the twentieth century as the age of the common man and woman but also the significance of an American past for the South. By reclaiming the South's American past, writers, historians, and scholars framed a South that stood for the democratic values of the American farmer—not for the aristocratic greed and licentiousness of planter society. Even more importantly, such a reframed and renewed past allowed southern literature to survive and to thrive, and to become one of the most distinct American literatures of the century.

1 Veins of Iron

ELLEN GLASGOW'S VIRGINIA FARMERS

Although many white southerners of Ellen Glasgow's time would have claimed that the Civil War was waged for traditional values, the war inadvertently also created what Lee Ann Whites has called a "gender crisis," with far-ranging implications for women. Between 1861 and 1865, southern white women found themselves displaced from the security of their homes, frequently to aid the war effort and oftentimes in search of work to help support their families. After the war, white women continued to be defined with stereotypes such as belle or southern lady, but these women increasingly found opportunities to express themselves as individuals outside the home, within community and church organizations and sometimes in the workplace. In moving beyond the home, however, the southern white woman faced a redefinition of her role within southern society. Although changes in women's status were not as quick to come about in the South as in the North, there were dissenting southern voices. By the turn of the century, for example, Kate Chopin was penning her novel *The Awakening* (1899), which evaluates the impossibilities of ideal models of southern womanhood. Chopin's "mother-women," her sheltering angels, followed traditional roles assigned to them by a southern patriarchy, but Edna, the novel's protagonist, was not at peace with those responsibilities and that identity. Grace King, too, was writing pieces such as "Bayou L'Ombre" in which she interprets the postwar South as a matriarchy, its men left impotent and ineffectual. By the turn of the century, some of the most significant writers of the South were moving away from the myths of the belle and the southern lady and toward redefinitions of southernness and womanhood.

Although Glasgow worked within a tradition of women's writing that pointed both to the necessity of offering new opportunities to women and to the failures that were likely to occur for women within a traditional southern framework, she was clearly of a later generation of writers. Unlike Chopin and King, Glasgow was greatly influenced by the figure of the New Woman of the 1890s and was involved in the suffrage movement in Virginia. Even in her earliest work, Glasgow addresses her concern with this new image of the southern woman—both her potential and the difficulties she faced.

The difficulties for the New Woman of the New South were fierce. In Glasgow's first published story, "A Woman of Tomorrow" (1895), a woman faces the conflict between her marriage and her career. Likewise, Glasgow's first two novels, *The Descendent* (1897) and *Phases of an Inferior Planet* (1898), tell of two women who move to New York City to escape a patriarchal southern society and to pursue artistic endeavors. Both women are plagued by unhappy marriages, but while one of Glasgow's heroines suffers through, the other leaves her husband for a singing job. Linda Wagner-Martin says that *The Descendent* examines Glasgow's early belief that "women—and their inherited attitudes and traditions—create their own tragedies" (24). *Phases of an Inferior Planet* deals with these same themes but blames women's condition more squarely on traditional patriarchal society.

The development of these themes is especially clear in Glasgow's later companion novels, *Virginia* (1913) and *Life and Gabriella* (1916). In these two novels, Glasgow paints a portrait of a woman's struggle for independence that is realistic and balanced, but she emphasizes the importance of a woman being able to make choices about her own life. In *Virginia,* for example, Virginia Pendleton, at age forty, realizes that her entire life has been the sum of her care for her husband and children. In *Life and Gabriella,* Gabriella's marriage to George Fowler, a wealthy New Yorker, ends in divorce after his drinking becomes a problem. In order to support herself, her children, and her in-laws, Gabriella works as a designer in New York and eventually becomes quite successful. Although she becomes an independent career woman out of necessity, she remains feminine and continues to show love for her children. When she meets Ben O'Hara, a wealthy railroad man, she decides to marry him, but in doing so she gives up some measure of what she has accomplished. Scholars read the ending of this novel with mixed reactions. On the one hand, Gabriella is able to choose marriage not out of necessity for financial support but instead because it is what she desires. On the other hand, in marrying, she sacrifices her selfhood.

As a whole, Glasgow's novels about southern women reflect a tension between what Glasgow termed "the sheltered life" and a "vein of iron." Both phrases she used again and again in her novels and eventually employed them as titles for two of her books. "The sheltered life" and a "vein of iron" suggest the tension between two roles for the southern woman: to be a pedestaled dependent like Eva Birdsong in *The Sheltered Life* or to exude strength that women like Dorinda and Ada have inherited from their mothers and grandmothers in *Barren Ground* (1925) and *Vein of Iron* (1935). In her writings, Glasgow points to the weaknesses and failures of the belle as a model for southern women. Instead, she favors a woman who is feminine yet who possesses the abilities to live her life as she chooses, to pursue her personal artistic endeavors, and to endure.

For Glasgow, the southern white woman had to be displaced from her pedestal in order for her to have control over her own life and her own identity. But in displacing the belle, Glasgow also had to find a new model. In southern literature, the southern white female had been traditionally defined by her beauty, her delicacy and frailties, her piety, and her chastity. The belle existed in the context of a plantation culture that viewed her as a companion to the male cavalier. Her goodness could be easily crushed if she were not guarded and controlled. Glasgow explains in *A Certain Measure* (1938) that as she wrote *Barren Ground*, the novel evolved as "a complete reversal of a classic situation." Dorinda is a betrayed woman, but instead of languishing in her prescribed role, she finds an inner strength that sustains her. According to Glasgow, in *Barren Ground* she created a unique and groundbreaking character: "For once, in Southern fiction, the betrayed woman would become the victor instead of the victim. In the end, she would triumph through that deep instinct for survival, which had ceased to be a negative quality and had strengthened into a dynamic force . . . And she would never lose her inner fidelity, that vital affirmation of life, 'I think, I feel, I am.' The only thing that mattered was her triumph over circumstances" (160). Dorinda's triumph, nevertheless, posed a problem for Glasgow as writer and as southern woman.

Glasgow redefined woman's role by looking back to the frontier past of Virginia. She outlines a model for this new woman in *Barren Ground* and *Vein of Iron,* an agrarian figure patterned after the yeoman farmer. For Glasgow, the yeoman farmer embodies strength for the South and for its women, for in order for a southern rural community to survive, women must take leadership roles in their families. In *Barren Ground,* Glasgow suggests that in order for the southern woman to regain her humanity she must have the independence and self-sustaining qualities of her ancestors, the pioneer-yeomen who settled and first planted the southern earth. In more general terms, she suggests that in order to rejuvenate the soil, in order to renew southern culture, the modern southerner must draw upon the yeoman past for individual power and courage.

This model, found within the roots of southern history, was formulated from the southern frontier past. Glasgow suggests that the South was in decline during the postbellum period partly because of its failure in war and its abuse during Reconstruction. Clearly, she also sees the results of the disintegration of yeoman values in the South in her formulation. In *A Certain Measure,* Glasgow contrasts a "higher class," in which "the spirit of adventure had disintegrated into an evasive idealism, a philosophy of heroic defeat," with what she calls the "more backward rural group" whose "fortitude had degenerated into a condition of moral inertia." Yet, as she explains, the "rural group" of southerners had "sprung from the oldest roots in American soil." Making careful note that she was not considering Native Americans, Glasgow says that in digging for these roots, we can discover "the raw stuff of American civilization, the beginning and, one is tempted to add, the end of American democracy" (155). Calling herself a "psychological novelist," Glasgow addresses two questions: "Was this culture actually dying? Was the wasting malady incurable?" She concludes that it is "the Virginian strain, the American fibre"— that is, the "innate capacity to exist without living, to endure without enjoying"—that provides Dorinda with the fortitude and willingness to triumph. As a descendent of the Scotch-Irish and the English "conquerors of the wilderness," Dorinda owes her instinct for survival to the yeomen who came before her (156).

Glasgow identifies the yeomanry as a "special rural class" that she believes has not yet been the focus of fictional literature. Defining this "special" class as farmers, she says that this group of southerners—"a buffer class between the opulent gentry and the hired labourers"— has been misidentified in the past. They were not poor whites, for they owned property, albeit land that was depleted from overuse and often left untilled. Glasgow alludes to their "liberal part in the making of Southern history." Distinguishing between the yeoman farmer and the aristocrat, she says that this special class has been known as the "good people," while the aristocrat has been said to be of "good family" (157–58). She claims for the "good people" an inheritance reaching back to the English yeomanry. Describing the ancestors of the Abernathy and the Pedlar families in *Barren Ground,* in particular, she says that they "had felled trees and built log cabins and withstood the red man on the Virginian frontier. Some of them had followed the westward trail of the Indian, and had won back, step by step, the vanishing border beyond the Shenandoah. They had fought in the French and Indian Wars and throughout the Revolution, and they had stacked their muskets for the last time at Appomattox. In pioneer days, they were the men in buckskin; they were the lone fighters; they were the sharp-shooters; they were the long hunters" (157).

Although they were the ones who settled the land and established a farming class in the South, the "good people" were invisible in history. They have not had a voice, Glasgow says, and they had no literary voice to speak for them. Glasgow sought to change that, and to speak for the yeomen. She came from similar stock. Her father, Francis Thomas Glasgow, was born in western Virginia and was of Scottish and Irish descent. While Glasgow viewed her mother, who came from an aristocratic family of Tidewater Virginia, as gentle and delicate, she described her father as "stalwart, unbending, rock-ribbed with Calvinism" (*The Woman Within*, 16).

In *Barren Ground*, Dorinda has inherited from her ancestors before her "a kinship with the solid earth under her feet, a long communion with the inanimate dust" (158). Like the vein of iron that takes on life in the furrows of the field, a large pine tree represents for Dorinda the endurance of her father. As her father lies on his deathbed, he looks out the window at a pine tree and the open sky. At first, Dorinda asks if the sunshine coming in the window bothers him, but she soon realizes how much the pine on the hill means to him. When Nathan suggests she consider timbering the pine on the hill, Dorinda exclaims, "It's the only thing Pa likes to watch now. He loves it." Nathan can understand: "I like a big tree myself." Dorinda's mother believes that the tree means "more to him than anything human" (296). "Sometimes in stormy weather that pine is like a rocky crag with the sea beating against it," Dorinda explains. The big pine tree possesses "all the meaning of [their] life . . . all the meaning of the country. Endurance, that's what it is" (268). After her father's death, Dorinda says she will wait to cut down the tallest of the trees on the property until it becomes a necessity. As she says to herself, "It would be slaughter" (299).

Glasgow's Virginia farmer is in many ways a traditional yeoman but also carries the mark of outside influence, a characteristic in some ways in conflict with the traditional yeoman farmer's independence. Glasgow's yeoman is, however, a woman who represents a matriarchal pattern. She is part of a family unit that works the soil together. Dorinda labors alongside her hired hands, as the pre–Civil War yeoman would have done. Both Dorinda and Ada farm in order to keep their families alive.

The South Dorinda was born into had been impoverished by the Civil War and Reconstruction, and by the tenant farming system, tobacco farming that left the soil sterile, the lack of hired labor, and the South's general inability to nurture the land. Dorinda believes, too, that the "instinct to slight" has ruined the South. "Indigenous to the soil of the South," she says, this instinct has tempted her during the long hours of work when it seemed as if it would be easier "to be swift and casual than to be slow and thorough." She is able to hold back the impulse to neglect her work through carelessness or inattention (302–3). Ultimately, she takes Old Matthew's advice: "Put yo' heart in the land. The land is the only thing that will stay by you" (323).

Glasgow titles the sections of her novel with the names of plants that grow from the depleted soil of Dorinda's Virginia, plants that only grow in the poorest of soils: broomsedge, pine, and life-everlasting. Even though Dorinda's family owns a thousand acres, they are called "land poor," for though they own land, they are not able to cultivate it productively. He was a man born in the wrong time, Dorinda says about her father, whom she believed did all he could to help sustain the land and ultimately gave his life for the land. He was alone in his work on the farm, and the farm finally ate up his strength to conquer him.

Even Jason, Dorinda's love interest, recognizes how important it is for a farmer to have a close relationship to the soil and remain aware of the needs of the earth. Tenants, he says, have treated the land as "a stingy man uses a horse he has hired by the month." Even farmers have "worked and starved the land to a skeleton" (111). But in understanding what the soil needs, the farmer can make decisions about the best ways to work the earth. Instead of raising tobacco, for example, Dorinda is better served to raise stock or dairy cattle on her property. Although Jason seems to have some insight into the situation, he is both literally and figuratively overcome by the broomsedge. He does not possess the strength and endurance that lead Dorinda to success. She is ultimately able to buy Jason's family farm because of her marriage to Nathan, one of the few men in the community who recognizes the importance of using modern farming methods and equipment. "One man ain't a team," Nathan says of Dorinda's father's inability to rejuvenate his farm. He is referring not only to labor issues but also to familial effort in revitalizing the soil. Instead of standing symbolically for the land, Glasgow's women possess it and care for it as one would a child. The land has been passed down to Dorinda through her mother's family rather than her father's. And while the possession of land brings with it suffering, it is through the land that Dorinda finds her ability to survive. The emptiness of this landscape also reflects the loneliness of Dorinda's life. Yet in building an emotional attachment to the soil, she at once finds a release from her feelings of heartbreak and a means of connecting with her ancestors, her parents, Fluvanna, Nathan, and her community. Hard work seemed to lead her parents nowhere but to the grave, but for Dorinda it brings a life of satisfaction and fulfillment.

Devastated by Jason's marriage to Geneva Ellgood, Dorinda finds the will to survive in the vein of iron that she carries from her ancestors who first settled the farm. Until the night of a classical music concert and a stroll by the park in New York City, she could only associate Old Farm with the image of Jason. But the vein of iron that connected her to a familial past was much deeper than the emotions she held for Jason. Something was pulling her back to the land:

> For the first time she could think of Old Farm without invoking the image of Jason. For the first time since she had left home, she felt that earlier and deeper associations were reaching out to her, that they were groping after her, like the tendrils of vines, through the darkness and violence of her later memories. Earlier and deeper associations, rooted there in the earth, were drawing her back across time and space and forgetfulness. Passion stirred again in her heart; but it was passion transfigured, recoiling from the personal to the impersonal object. It seemed to her, walking there in the blue twilight, that the music had released some imprisoned force in the depths of her being, and that this force was spreading out over the world, that it was growing wider and thinner until it covered all the desolate country at Old Farm. With a shock of joy, she realized that she was no longer benumbed, that she had come to life again. She had come to life again, but how differently! (239)

Dorinda tells Doctor Burch that she hears the farm calling her back home to care for it. That night, she dreams of plowing the soil of Old Farm, but she plows fields of thistles, all wearing Jason's face. Despite this nightmare that revisits her, Dorinda believes that the land holds a promise of renewal in the rejuvenated cycles of the seasons, in the sown grain, in the continuity of harvests ripening in the fields.

Glasgow also speaks of the sacrifices that Dorinda must make for the earth. Dorinda has the "old feeling" that the land thinks and feels and has "a secret personal life of its own" (268). She believes that she belongs to the land, but whatever she gives to the land—even herself—will always be hers. Only in giving herself fully to its care can she ultimately find that sense of renewal within herself so that she might renew the soil. As Glasgow explains, the land can only be restored if Dorinda "enrich[es] the land with her abundant vitality." Her desire to bring about this change in the landscape is an all-consuming passion. Yet as Glasgow shows the intimacy of Dorinda's relationship with the land, she also speaks of Dorinda's triumph over the abandoned fields. She has to suffer and toil as the pioneers once did after they "snatched a home from the wilderness" (397). But it is because those pioneers triumphed that Dorinda can bring life to the abandoned fields. By giving herself to the land and to life, she is able to live to the fullest in her agrarian existence.

Dorinda's vein of iron is not only the inherited strength that runs in her veins but also what she has "gleaned from those heavy furrows of her great-grandfather's sowing." Glasgow points to the qualities of the yeoman farmer that support Dorinda: "firmness of purpose, independence of character, courage of living" (411). Although Glasgow partly attributes Dorinda's strength to the Presbyterianism of her ancestors, she is quick to clarify that it was neither religion nor philosophy—"nothing outside of her own being"—that had "delivered her from evil." Dorinda's vein of iron was "merely the instinct older than herself, stronger than circumstances, deeper than the shifting surface of emotion." And that instinct said, "I will not be broken." Although the worlds of what Glasgow calls "the covenant" might change, "the ancient mettle still infused its spirit" (460). Glasgow believed that modern southerners, facing the hardships of a region not as economically advanced as the rest of the United States, might find value in the original spirit of the southern pioneers—a spirit of adventure, of endurance, of persistence, and of courage.

Glasgow was also careful to suggest that the South must not remain in isolation. In an essay published in *The Reviewer*, Glasgow describes "the law of progress as superior to the rules of precedent" (48). *Barren Ground*, likewise, shows the farmer reaching beyond the limits of the farm in supporting the farm. Such a revival would be impossible without Dorinda's journey to the city, where she both recognizes the importance of the land to her life and the necessity of gaining knowledge of farming practices and borrowing money to begin the process of rejuvenation. It takes a team effort to revitalize the farm. In New York, Doctor Burch refers her to books that will ultimately help her learn a more scientific method of farming. Doctor Faraday tells her that like medicine, agriculture is also a science. It is because of his concern for her, his awareness of farming, and his appreciation for the care Dorinda gives his daughter that he and his wife provide Dorinda with the money to support her farming endeavors.

There are also successful farmers in Dorinda's community, such as James Ellgood, who has used phosphates and nitrate of soda and grown cowpeas to turn under in order to improve his soil. With help, she is ultimately able to produce at her dairy a product that is of high quality and will bring a good price. She sells her butter to a Washington, DC, hotel. Although commercialization does become, then, an important aspect of her life on the farm, this fact is only the reality of her situation in the twentieth century. She can ultimately sustain herself as farmer, but she must exist within the larger world. As Dorinda concludes, "If experience had taught her nothing else, it had at least made her a realist. She had learned to take things as they are." Like other members of Glasgow's modern yeomanry, Dorinda possesses the ability to control her own life: "As long as she could rule her own mind she was not afraid of the forces without" (252).

Dorinda reconstructs Old Farm within a maternal framework, and in doing so, she also ensures the farm's survival. By deciding to raise dairy cattle and chickens, Dorinda relies on the female animals and products associated with their female reproductive systems—milk and eggs—for her farm's survival. Dorinda depends, too, upon her mother's knowledge of white leghorn chickens. Ma knows them so well that she can identify the white leghorns as individuals, an ability Dorinda does not possess. The products of her farm are symbols of fertility rather than of poverty, of growth rather than of futility.

Dorinda also utilizes the traditional skills she possesses as a woman in order to run her farm: housekeeping and cleaning. She knows the importance of seeing that her cows are kept clean and brushed, and the stalls are "free from a speck of dirt" (287). As James Elgood's son Bob tells her, it is important to keep the cows free of disease and to prevent contagious abortion. Dorinda identifies cleanliness as a feminine quality. She hires women milkers because, as Glasgow explains, Dorinda was "inspired by a firm though illogical belief in their superior neatness" (408). Other farmers—that is, male ones—believe that "cleanliness is a joke," but as a woman, whose tasks have been generally associated with the care, comfort, and tidiness of a household, Dorinda recognizes the need for an orderly, healthy environment. Inside the house, Dorinda doesn't like the parlor, even though the walls are covered with her great-grandfather's books. She wonders if perhaps she could "turn the room into a more comfortable and cheerful place" (368)

Dorinda shows her individual nature, too, in her decisions concerning the milking itself. The cows she purchases have never been milked by a woman. But instead of hiring a man to milk the cows and despite her mother's statement that she hoped nobody would see Dorinda, Dorinda dons overalls and does the milking herself. "You can't farm in skirts," she tells her mother (296). Actually, Dorinda attributes this decision to common sense. She will milk her cows her own way. "I'm the only person, man or woman, in the county" with common sense, she tells her mother (296). Every detail of the operation comes under her eye because she fears her workers will be careless. She works harder than everyone else, putting in longer hours and working with care and with an aim toward perfection. In giving herself fully to the land, Dorinda is able to achieve what many cannot. Ma points to Dorinda's brother Rufus who leaves his work to cut down a honey tree in order to satisfy his sweet tooth; not many men are able to put their individual wishes aside, Ma explains. Dorinda has the strength to set aside hers.

By rejuvenating the farm on her own terms, Dorinda also gains the respect of local farmers, especially Bob Ellgood who is also a dairy farmer. Dorinda is aware that although Bob was originally attracted to her physically, he has a greater admiration of her as a successful farmer. In recognizing that a man can have a "keen, impersonal admiration" of her as he might of another man, Dorinda concludes that although "the sensation was without the excitement of sex vanity, she found that it was quite as gratifying, and, she suspected, more durable." She believes she is being judged by her character, which pleases her. "I hope you'll make a success of it," Bob tells her. "I like women who take hold of things and aren't afraid of work when they have to do it. That's the right spirit" (285). Bob contrasts her with Jason, which pleases her greatly: "His laziness is bred in the bone, and he's the sort that will let apples rot on the ground rather than pick them up" (286). By the end of the novel, Bob is a marriage prospect following the death of his wife.

Dorinda's relationship with Fluvanna, a black woman she has hired to work with her, reflects the relationship of the yeoman to the African American. The best years of Dorinda's youth, according to Glasgow, were spent with Fluvanna on the isolated farm. Their feelings for each other were "as strong and elastic as the bond that holds relatives together": "They knew each other's daily lives; they shared the one absorbing interest in the farm; they trusted each other without discretion and without reserve" (339–40). Glasgow attempts to portray a relationship of equality, but she also suggests that although Dorinda has a great attachment to her servant, she could not forget the "feeling of condescension" that she had inherited from her southern ancestors (340).

Barren Ground suggests the possibilities of living the yeoman life in Dorinda's acceptance of Nathan because of the "bond of sympathy" they possess in farming (270). "Why was it so difficult, she wondered, to bring people to accept either a new idea or a new object?" (409). Nathan is the only man in the community who is willing to look toward the future instead of living in the past. He recognizes the value of machines like the telephone and the separator. He envisions a time when they will have an electric plant on the farm to aid in the milking and the separating. Dorinda views Nathan in life as dull but necessary. Yet with his death, when Nathan becomes a hero in the community by giving his life for others, he seems to suggest a greater value to Dorinda. He has sacrificed as she is sacrificing for the soil.

After Nathan's death, Dorinda lives, as Glasgow explains, "the richest and happiest" years of her life (446). Glasgow points to the value of the farmer's task beyond the limits of the home place as she explains how World War I was won with the help of the farmer. This war was unlike the Civil War, which brought only poverty and starvation, and left a "flame-like vividness" in the memories of Dorinda's mother. For Dorinda, this war was "no nearer . . . than a battle in history," but she could feel as if she played a part when she could see "victory in terms of crops, not battles" (446).

By the end of the novel, then, as Dorinda looks back to her life from middle age, she believes she can face the future "without romantic glamour, but . . . with integrity of vision." Although Glasgow emphasizes Dorinda's ability to see her world realistically, her view on the agrarian landscape is tinged with idealism. The difficulties and troubles of farming had "passed over her like wild geese" (461–62). Problems with finding adequate labor had been eased with the use of electricity and gasoline. Her name was becoming known throughout the state among the farmers. Her dairy products were bringing a high price on the market: "The best of life, she told herself with clear-eyed wisdom, was ahead of her. She saw other autumns like this one, hazy, bountiful in harvests, mellowing through the blue sheen of air into the red afterglow of winter; she saw the coral-tinted buds of the spring opening into the profusion of summer; and she saw the rim of the harvest moon shining orange-yellow through the boughs of the harp-shaped pine. Though she remembered the time when loveliness was like a sword in her heart, she knew now that where beauty exists the understanding soul can never remain desolate" (510). When John Abner reminds her of the possibilities of marriage to a local farmer, Dorinda quickly brushes off the prospect, saying, "I am thankful to have finished with all that" (511). She has obtained an individualism that might at times leave her in loneliness, but through it she has achieved a sense of purpose, a connection to the southern earth and to her heritage, and opportunities to look forward.

Although when Glasgow finished *Barren Ground,* she believed it would be her last novel, she reexamines these same possibilities for renewal in *Vein of Iron,* which was published in 1935. She was, as she explains in *A Certain Measure,* "after an excursion into civilized comedy," recovering the "substance and manner" of *Barren Ground* and of the novels before, which she says were written "in ardent revolt from a literary convention that was formalized and inflexible" (178–79). Once again she attempted to create a southern scene that avoided the romantic fallacy of literature of the turn of the century that the population of the South was comprised largely of aristocrats and black slaves. Framing this new novel within the context of the modernist struggle with industrialization, Glasgow asks, "Would they sink, in the end, under the dead weight of an age that believed only in the machine?" (168). Would her pioneer-Scots ancestors have been able to endure in the modern world? Would their descendents? In trying to answer these questions she looks not to a single individual, but instead she chronicles a family, focusing on the human ability to survive in the face of the forces that threaten civilization.

Set in the years leading up to the collapse of the stock market and in the Great Depression, the book examines the potential for American culture to survive one of the bitterest periods of U.S. history. On a universal level, the book concentrates on the struggle for sustenance and the vein of iron that helps modern human beings survive. Glasgow suggests that southerners—and more generally Americans—have lost that vein of iron possessed by their ancestors that helped them survive the settlement of the North American continent. According to the book's protagonist, Ada, her grandmother would have dismissed this post–World War II generation, calling them a "puny breed."

For Glasgow, the pioneers with their values and goals seem valuable models for those caught in a collapsing social system. She suggests in *A Certain Measure* that lives of "immobility" will collapse. She believes, too, that the "living germ" of the "long tradition of fortitude" that finds its roots in the frontier spirit is the only means of survival (178–79). "Simple folk," as Ada's grandmother calls the Fincastles, were descended from pioneers who out of necessity possessed an ability to rebuild from the ruins of life's tragedies. In many ways, Glasgow's pioneers are spiritual kin to Willa Cather's characters. Glasgow's pioneer has the courage to seek and to search, to discover new worlds and possibilities. And out of that search comes survival. Glasgow asks, for example, "Was this endless seeking an inheritance from the past?

Was it a survival of the westward thrust of the pioneer?" (51). The resourceful pioneer must venture forth without clear road passages as he makes his thrust into the wilderness. There were those who "rose superior to destiny," despite the harshness of their living conditions and the wilderness that surrounded them (424–45). Ada carries that potential in her blood.

To return to those original values, human beings must retreat to the land for strength and sustenance. For the first several weeks after the death of his wife, Mary Evelyn, Ada's father "turned to the hoe and the spade as an appeasement of grief." When the school year began again, he returned to the parlor for his classes, to what Glasgow describes as "the lonely work of his lifetime" (184–85). Ada even suggests that an equality comes from the human relationship to the earth. When she sees her father and a child that Glasgow describes as a "small colored urchin" both digging in the earth, Ada cries out, "Side by side . . . and it doesn't make the slightest difference to the earth that one is a philosopher and the other a piccaninny!" (249). Despite the clear racism of her statement, Ada still manages to see the common bond that the earth provides.

Those values that connect the family to the land reach back to their Scotch-Irish roots and to the family's migration to America. Glasgow recounts a lineage for the Fincastles that reaches back to County Donegal in Ireland. Ada knows the story of her family quite well, so well that it has reached mythic proportions in her mind, as well as for those in her family and community. Pastor John Fincastle, Ada's great-great-great-grandfather, had brought with him a few members of his congregation and the elders and deacons of his church from County Donegal to Ulster, where his flock set out on a voyage across the Atlantic to Philadelphia. They remained in Pennsylvania for a few years but eventually the heartier ones among them decided to move to Virginia. Led by John Fincastle, who was then known as the "scholar pioneer" because he carried with him not only his Bible but as many other books as he could take in his pack, the group took the Indian Road into Virginia.

After discovering the Virginia settlements were too hostile to those who desired a "peace with his Maker," John Fincastle and his flock decided once again to thrust out into the frontier. Glasgow says, "the wilderness flowed into him and ebbed back again." Fincastle was following "the dream of a free country, the dream of a country so vast that each man would have room to bury his dead on his own land" (20). These hardy pioneers had nothing to follow, for the pioneers before them had left no trails or even footprints to follow through Indian territory. Their only guide was the sun and sometimes the subtle marks left by Indian hunters. The pioneers found their own way through the wilderness and carried with them only the barest of necessities. Wagons could not make their way into the wilderness, so they were forced to carry what they took with them on horseback. When John Fincastle and his flock arrived in the area of what would be the town of Ironside, they built the old stone church with their bare hands and settled down as farmers.

At certain moments, Ada seems to recognize the value of living with these people as her models. At times, flashes of insight, of comfort, come to her, but until the end of the book, when she and her husband make the decision to settle in Ironside, there isn't that peace for her that comes through understanding. "Suddenly, without reason, the meaning that sometimes starts out of life and seems to make everything clear and simple flashed back at her from the valley, the stream, the mountains, the sky. An instant only, and then it was gone, like the flight of an eagle" (249). So it is for much of the book. Again and again, though, the strength of her blood sustains her. She connects the travail of her own life with her ancestors' grief and then ultimate strength. Her grandmother reminds her that she has "strong blood" and that she should never let that blood be weakened, for "Thin blood runs to wickedness" (21).

As her grandmother told the stories of the difficulties faced by John Fincastle and his flock, her words would "drop thick and fast, like the pelting of hail." Ada's "flesh crawled with fear that was somehow delicious" as she heard the story of Mrs. Ettrick, a woman her grandmother described as of great strength, who was "surprised by a redskin" as she forded the creek while gathering sand for the mortar to build the church. She killed him with a single blow from her hatchet and then rode her horse back to the settlement where she warned the armed men of her community of the enemy presence (18–21). Or the story of a man who lived near her grandfather who, when others from the community took refuge in the stockade during an Indian attack, instead held his cabin. Within ten years time, he had lost two wives and two families of children to Indian attacks. Or the story of Martha Tod, who was kidnapped by Indians and married a young chief. When her brothers came to redeem her and killed her husband, she wept because her husband had been a noble and virtuous man. She never entrusted her story of life among the Indians to anyone. "Time and again, they had risen from the ruins of happiness," Glasgow says of the Fincastles and their neighbors, "Yet they had gone on; they had rebuilt the ruins; they had scattered life more abundantly over the ashes" (40–41).

When the young Ada finds herself pregnant by Ralph, she walks over the hillside outside of Ironside trying to find some strength for all that she knows is coming with the birth of her child. Feeling her child move within her, Ada sees the child as possessing a "strange like knit to her own and thrusting up from the depths of her being toward a destiny that would be separate and different" (247). As she looks out over the sheep pasture, Smiling Creek, and the willows, the water of the creek ripples as the wind blows across its surface, and the light reflected in the water is broken with the leaves that the water carries. To comfort herself that her world is not too difficult to bear, she reminds herself that other women have suffered through greater difficulties. Ada focuses on that light when she feels afraid and out of control. To find peace, she gazes on the water and the willows, thinking about all that those first settlers on Smiling Creek were forced to endure just to live. They never lost the will to live, she tells herself. Once again those stories of tragedy and blood come to her. The pioneers were heroic in their fortitude. Ada remembers the story of Mrs. Morecock who was held captive by Indians: "Mrs. Morecock had seen the brains of her baby spatter her skirts; she had been famished for food as a captive; she had eaten roots; when she reached water, she had knelt down and lapped it up like an animal. In the end she had had the courage to escape, she had crossed trackless mountains on her way home to Ironside. For months she had lived on berries and the bark of black gum or sassafras. Though she was a walking skeleton when she reached Ironside, she had had the spirit, or the folly, to begin life again" (248).

Ada wonders if the present exists in isolation from the past. Or does that "vein of iron" link the generations in strength? "Sitting there, in touch with the land that had been won from the wilderness, she braced her own strength against that endurance, that hardness. How had her Great-great-grandmother Tod felt when she bore her child in the wigwam of a savage? What was her own plight to that? Oh, but the wilderness! If only she might hide away and have her child on a bed of pine boughs!" (248). Later, when Ada is in labor, she feels the strength of her grandmother's arms around her. Pressed tight to a bosom that seems "as stout as oak, as sustaining as fortitude," Ada feels her grandmother's "large, strong, knotted, healing" hand as it pushes back her wet hair from her forehead. The line of her ancestors also gives her strength as "the steadfast life of the house, the strong fibers, the closely knit generations [gather] above, around, underneath." She feels comforted, knowing that her ancestors provide a sort of safety net underneath her, as the memory of their strength cradles and secures her (260).

The intense desire to return to the mountain becomes the focal point of the end of the novel. Although Ada and Ralph find themselves living in a Queenborough community of simple folk who like them have been drawn to the city by a money economy that promises survival, Ada recognizes the dangers of the encroaching industrialization, mechanization, and commercialism of the modern world. When Ranny says he wants a radio, Ada tells him they are saving for the Manse. When Ranny, whose friend's family has recently bought a car, asks what installment means, Ada responds, "It means buying what you can't afford" (324). Glasgow clearly suggests that the southerner must return to rural life in order to survive. While they live in the city, Ada holds on to a secret dream of returning to Ironside, where she believes she has "left a part of [herself], perhaps only a root, in the Valley." It is not her intention to return immediately, but to wait until she and Ralph are older and have saved some money (290). Away from the valley, however, as time passed and separated her from her memories, she still pictures herself walking, running, rising, and stooping in the valley, but then that image of herself in a light blue dress disappears, "a shadow among shadows, within the hyacinth-colored circle of mountains." But as that image disappeared, so, too, did her self. Here, now, in Queenborough, she is a "single cell of experience" but she also remains ever hopeful that she might return to the valley and to the life she and her ancestors had known there (314).

The pull of the Great Valley seems as great for Ada's father as it does for Ada. While he was away, the Great Valley seemed as if it "might be upon another planet, so distant, so luminously green and springlike did it appear in his memory." His recollections of the place were always set in the springtime. Sometimes, though, "the thrilling blue of God's Mountain" seemed as if it were a place that could only exist within his mind. But in existing there within his mind, it was part of his very being, part of his soul. At other times, however, he saw himself drifting on "a vast plain, treeless and dead, where all the peaks had been leveled" as the twilight was "flowing down in a sultry, impalpable tide" (295). John Fincastle also possesses a driving desire to return to Ironside—but to be buried. He claims a practical purpose in returning: he will be able to help his family because the cost of burial will be less. But "only in Ironside could he find the freedom to sink back into changeless beatitude, into nothing and everything" (452). He feels a timeless connection to the place, believing that human beings always continue to exist within the places where they are born.

When Ralph suggests they are living in the past by clinging to family roots, Ada knows better. She believes that life in the valley will return them to the values that will help them endure the difficulties they have faced in the city. They plan to raise vegetables. Aunt Meggie, Ada suggests, can raise chickens, and they can produce their garden from seeds they have gathered the year before. Ada can also do some part-time work as a dressmaker. Ralph points out that there is much work to do, and that they might be "peasants." Using the term disparagingly, Ralph and Ada both seem to connect the term with survival—not endurance. Ada responds to Ralph, for example, by saying, "Nothing can make peasants of us but ourselves. Grandmother had less when she grew up, but she wasn't a peasant. Living with the savages didn't turn Great-great-grandmother Tod into a savage." How much they have in comparison to the first Fincastles, she points out. "What would he have thought if he had stumbled upon a brick house, a garden with seeds in the ground, a well, a springhouse, and the whole of Smiling Creek, with no Indians in the willows?" Ralph, however, suggests there is a difference in the way human beings now view their world and the way they did as pioneers. The pioneer, Ralph says, "had not only civilization, but Heaven and Hell, within himself." In an almost chiding manner, he adds, "It takes conviction to set out to despoil the wilderness, defraud Indians of their hunting-grounds, and start to build a new Jerusalem for predestinarians" (460).

Although Ada responds to Ralph by asking him not to be bitter about the lives they have led in the city, she can encourage him to imagine and make real a life of hopefulness rather than one of pity because of what she has taken from her ancestors' memory: "She had a sense, more a feeling than a vision, of the dead generations behind her. They had come to life there in the past; they were lending her their fortitude; they were reaching out to her in adversity. This was the heritage they had left. She could lean back on their strength; she could recover that lost certainty of a continuing tradition" (461). When Ralph calls Ada a "dreamer," saying, "It's queer that a dreamer should be a rock to lean on," Glasgow describes the couple as "in the brilliant sunlight, surrounded by the pale green of the landscape." Ralph's face is "the face of an old man—creased, hardened, hollowed, and stained by time" (461), but Ada is surrounded by hope and peace. "With a sudden glow of surprise," Ada thinks, "Never, not even when we were young . . . was it so perfect as this" (462).

To be sure, Glasgow's work after the publication of *Vein of Iron* was molded and shaped by her achievements in *Barren Ground* and *Vein of Iron*. Her Virginia farmers are women of strength who sustain themselves by looking back to their southern roots, not a South of belles and plantations but of the pioneer women and men who originally settled the land. By first examining both the freedoms and hardships experienced by the yeoman farmers who built the South, Glasgow was able to move on to *In This Our Life* (1941), which Helen Fiddyment Levy says allowed her to find "refuge in a visionary pastoral home place presided over by an elder wise woman, an American icon" (221).

Glasgow's achievement as a writer would also have a sweeping influence on other southern writers of her period and of later generations. Called "the first really modern Southern novelist, the pioneer" by Louis D. Rubin in his introduction to *Ellen Glasgow: Centennial Essays* (1976), she had a direct, clear influence on a wealth of writers (Katherine Anne Porter and Eudora Welty, in particular) who crafted women characters who are at home in the world—not isolated from it. Glasgow's women are empowered by their roles as pioneers, as settlers, as tillers of the earth. They are set free through attachments to a southern earth that Glasgow reconfigured to tell of a woman's power rather than of her weakness. Ellen Glasgow left southern women writers a legacy that reconstructs the framework assigned to women—a southern landscape not limited to the southern belle but expanded to include the new possibilities of southern womanhood.

2 The Agrarians

TAKING THEIR STAND

"Suddenly we realized to the full what we had long been dimly feeling, that the Lost Cause might not be wholly lost after all. In its very backwardness the South had clung to some secret which embodied, it seemed, the elements out of which its own reconstruction—and possibly even the reconstruction of America—might be achieved" (Rubin, "Introduction," *I'll Take My Stand,* xxv–xxvi). In these words, Donald Davidson framed the conflict between northern industrialization and southern agrarianism not only as a second civil war between the North and the South, but also as a fight for the survival of American society—and humanity at large. According to Davidson and the other Agrarians (a group that included such formidable literary figures as Allen Tate, John Crowe Ransom, Andrew Lytle, and Robert Penn Warren), the nation had to decide between two paths: industrial or agrarian. The South might have lost on the battlefields of the Civil War, but America faced a national dilemma and the South offered a promising answer for the country as a whole. Writing years later Tate explained that he and John Crowe Ransom came to the same conclusions rather serendipitously: "And then one day—I cannot be sure of the year, I think 1926—I wrote John Ransom a new sort of letter. I told him that we must do something about Southern history and the culture of the South. John had written, on the same day, the same message to me" ("The Fugitive," 34). The result was *I'll Take My Stand,* a collection of essays that outlines the qualities of a rural South that the Agrarians believed offered possibilities for renewal for a country entering the Great Depression.

The writer-friends who were at the center of the Agrarian movement originally found their way together at Vanderbilt University, where they and others of like mind gathered at the home of Sidney Mittron Hirsch for discussions on poetry. Not officially connected to the university (as the point is always made), the group of writers, including Warren, Ransom, Tate, Davidson, and eventually Lytle, were all in some way connected to Vanderbilt either as students or as instructors. All of them came to Nashville with roots in the Upper South of Tennessee or Kentucky. As poets, they sponsored the publication of a little magazine, *The Fugitive*, which has traditionally been assigned a prominent place in the beginning of the Southern Renaissance. Published from 1922 until 1925, the magazine attracted the attention of writers and editors far beyond the South, yet the preface to the first number claimed a very personal objective. In establishing their publication, the editors claimed their explicit desire to "flee the high-caste Brahmins of the Old South." By reawakening southern literature and interest in the arts, these Fugitive writers have assumed the role of literary fathers in many of the histories and anthologies of southern literature.

With the 1930 publication of *I'll Take My Stand*, the members of this group proclaimed an agrarian, as opposed to industrial, way of life by specifically linking agrarianism with the South and an industrial life with the North. The tremendous impact of this book is unquestionable, although recent discussions on the history of southern literature suggest that a full assessment of its influence is only now coming forth. Michael Kreyling, for example, argues in his book *Inventing Southern Literature* that the Agrarians and their conservatism retain an overshadowing influence in southern literary scholarship. *I'll Take My Stand* quite clearly remains a book to reckon with, despite the fact that readings of southern literature are now much more far-ranging and inclusive than they were even ten years ago.

Writing "to support a Southern way of life against what may be called the American or prevailing way," as the much-quoted line goes, the Agrarians hoped to preserve a way of life that they saw rapidly fading, one that their parents and grandparents before them had valued and protected because it represented for them the very foundations of a strong southern tradition. The sons and grandsons dared not lose another foothold for the South during a time when the region was just reentering the United States following World War I. On the one hand, the Agrarians saw significance in the South retaining its individuality from the rest of the country. But on the other, they suggested that the region had much to offer the rest of the United States. Their logic in proposing that agrarian values should supplant the burgeoning American ones seemed sound enough. The Agrarians emphasized in their statement of principles that the South—because of its agrarian roots—still possessed a "genuine humanism" and a culture based on a distinct tradition (Ransom, "Introduction," xliv). Other sections of the country possessed similar groundings, but like the South they were apt to lose that "genuine humanism" if the United States became an industrial rather than an agricultural nation.

Industrialization not only threatened the essential values of a society, according to the Agrarians, but it also dehumanized a society. In the "Statement of Principles" that introduces the collection of essays, industrialization is described as "a system that has so little regard for individual wants," one that places value in society as a whole rather than in the individual. *I'll Take My Stand* is clearly shaped by the necessity of guarding the American political foundation on individual human rights. Human beings, according to the "Statement of Principles," should not place an abstract social ideal before "their private dignity and happiness," for in doing so they place society before the individual. To do so was absurd, they explained, as a person's ultimate responsibility was for the care of himself and of his neighbor—"not for the hypothetical welfare of some fabulous creature called society" (Ransom, "Introduction," xlvi). The "Statement of Principles" thus clearly suggests that the American political experiment itself was in danger of failing if the country chose industrialization over agrarianism. The central struggle identified in the book seems to be the survival of America rather than the survival of the South. The critical argument lies not in southern isolationism but in the South's ability to guide the rest of the country—the South's ability to "rise again."

But what kind of a South did the Agrarians hold up as a model for the rest of the country? What exactly was the context of the secret to which the South had clung? The strategies outlined in the book are mixed. There are clear distinctions between the essays of Allen Tate, John Crowe Ransom, and John Gould Fletcher, which are typically described as elitist, and those written by Donald Davidson, Andrew Lytle, Herman Clarence Nixon, and Frank Owsley, which depict a yeoman tradition based on Jeffersonian agrarianism. At the heart of the book, then, is not only the conflict between North and South but also the central conflict between two basic ideologies: yeoman versus cavalier. The book itself remains an enigma because of this central issue that never seems to be resolved. Nevertheless, the "Statement of Principles" explains that the term "agrarian" is left undefined because the word "does not stand in particular need of definition" (xlvi). Their joint statement, however, rightly suggests the breadth of the authors' views even on this subject. The book also tends to focus on abstractions rather than on practical suggestions for formulating agrarian societies.

Although *I'll Take My Stand* is itself a conflicted book, the majority of the Agrarians ultimately came to support the ideal of the yeoman and thus the democratic values of the yeoman or the common man (and woman). In large part, the importance of the yeoman in the political writings of John Crowe Ransom and Allen Tate, in particular, was the result of the deepening economic depression, but the creative literature by the prominent members of the Agrarian group was also significantly influenced by the yeoman figure. The years following the publication of the book suggest a turn for Tate and Ransom to those more practical applications. Tate joined the Distributist movement, and Ransom published essays, such as his 1933 "Happy Farmers," that went so far as to suggest the U.S. government tax large farming equipment in order to keep farmers farming. The deepening depression intensified Tate and Ransom's opinions on agrarianism—at least for the time being—and refocused many of the Agrarians on the ideal of the yeoman.

I'll Take My Stand was not meant to be a practical guide to living the agrarian life, but it does suggest a growing awareness among its writers to claim for the South a new history. The yeoman was a figure that would allow for the South to take a prominent role in the future course of the United States. The Agrarians proposed a restoration of American society, but it was a restoration framed within a southern context. More specifically, the undercurrent of their efforts was to propose a southern solution to an American problem, a southern solution firmly tied to its American roots.

Although the core group of writers who came together as the Fugitive poets and then again to write the essays in *I'll Take My Stand* are now typically viewed as the establishment, they were, in fact, writers who were approaching their southernness from the fringes. I do not suggest that this group of white, male authors suffered any of the hardships and atrocities of African Americans in slavery or the political disenfranchisement of women, or that they would have perceived themselves as marginal. They did, nevertheless, approach the South from the border country. As Tennesseans and Kentuckians, they were citizens of a border South. Their South was not the Deep South or the mountain South, or the seaboard South of Virginia and the Carolinas, and indeed their South has sometimes been called a Third South. Although Tate probably felt this struggle most intensely, the others were certain to have experienced some degree of it.

Allen Tate's unfinished book, most aptly titled *Ancestors of Exile,* exemplifies this conflict. But its failure is also telling. The idea for the manuscript revolves around a conflict that Tate's own mother created for him. Tate says in his essay "A Lost Traveler's Dream" that until he was thirty, he had not lived in one place longer than three years. Sometimes his family moved several times a year, "moving *away* from something my mother didn't like." Perhaps, though, saying that his mother "gradually withdrew from the world" was a better way of explaining it: "My mother gradually withdrew from the world, and withdrew me also, gradually, from the time I was a small boy; so that we might as well have been living, and I been born, in a tavern at a crossroads" (7). Tate's mother, Eleanor Varnell, had always told him that he had been born in Virginia. She emphasized that she was "descended from Jamestown" and "believed in heredity," and she saw to it that her sons made regular trips to Virginia to visit her family home places and relatives (10). Allen Tate did not discover until he was thirty years old that he was born in Kentucky rather than in Virginia, even though the rest of his family had known all along. As Tate says in "A Lost Traveler's Dream," "for men of my region and time one's birthplace was important"; Virginia was a more suitable place of birth than Kentucky (6).

The conflict between these two southern regions is reiterated by Lytle in a 1929 letter to Tate: "How can a Tennessean and Kentuckian return to Virginia? I have a suspicion that a Virginian doesn't differentiate much between one who comes from the North and one who comes from behind the blue ridge, and if he does, he will favor the carpetbagger to, shall I say, the scalawag" (Young and Sarcone 29). The division between Souths was perhaps even stronger between Upper and Deep. According to Tate's 1929 biography of Jefferson Davis, during the Civil War period, Kentucky and Tennessee were "as closely bound to Illinois and Indiana as to Alabama and Mississippi, more closely than to South Carolina and Georgia" (60). Tate explains that the cotton industry, "that unifier of Southern life," also distinguished the Deep South from the rest of the South. Indeed, as Tate speculates, without the enormous power of cotton in the Deep South, Virginia and Kentucky would have become part of the North. As a result, the Civil War never would have occurred (30–31).

By elevating the yeoman figure in their writings, the Agrarians placed much of the blame for the South's defeat in the Civil War firmly on the shoulders of the Deep South. Their mythologized figures took extreme forms, like Lytle's "devil" Forrest, the "defender" of Middle Tennessee and "wizard of the saddle." Portrayed by Lytle in his *Bedford Forrest and His Critter Company* (1931), this brave and valiant leader has horse after horse shot out from under him as he enlists the sun "to serve in his ranks" (296–97). Even though General Sherman believed that he could "whip" Forrest's infantry (336), Sherman said, "There will never be peace in Tennessee until Forrest is dead" (305). Although he was a fighter, not a philosopher, Lytle's Forrest could see beyond the cotton snobs and nouveaux riches of the Deep South. Lytle speculates Jefferson Davis forgot that he was born in a dog run and that "the backbone of the South and its armies was the plain people" (356–57). Forrest, by contrast, never forgot who he was and where he was born. Because he remembered, Forrest possessed the ability to revive enthusiasm in the war among the people. Despite Forrest's potential as a leader, Lytle suggests, the South ultimately lost the war in part because his leadership abilities were not as highly valued as Jefferson Davis's.

In many ways, Lytle's Nathan Bedford Forrest is reminiscent of his yeoman farmer in "The Hind Tit," his essay in *I'll Take My Stand.* Lytle's biography of Forrest describes a common man who never forgot his humble roots even as a Confederate general. Forrest was a product of the yeomanry, and Lytle raises him up as an example of what a man who is reared with these roots can accomplish. By the time of Bedford Forrest's youth, many settlers seemed to have forgotten Thomas Jefferson's admonition that only a small piece of land was necessary to live a good life. People were more interested in growing cotton and becoming wealthy than in living a life close to the soil. When his father died, Bedford became head of the household. As Lytle says, "Under [his mother] Mariam's eye Bedford did more than support her. His axe rang surer, the fence rails stood squarer, and the new ground grubbed cleaner than ever before." Mariam Forrest's children were obedient; they had to be for the family to survive. There was much to be done around the household: yarn had to be spun, woven into cloth, and then sewn into clothing; game had to be killed and the meat salted down and smoked; corn had to be grown, harvested, and sent to the mill; candles and soap had to be made and fruit dried. "So hard were they pushed," according to Lytle, "that the young Bedford often sat down by candlelight to make shoes and buckskin leggings for his brothers. Lytle says that Forrest was always proud of his self-sufficiency: "Barely turned a man, with no experience in family matters, to take from the new ground and forests their victuals and with his own hands to make their shoes, gave him a sense of achievement he was never to feel again" (17).

John Bradbury notes in his book *The Fugitives: A Critical Account* (1958) that Tate also distinguished between Upper and Deep South traditions in order to support his thesis that Jefferson Davis was "inadequa[te] to his function," while Stonewall Jackson was "adequate." In his biography of Davis, Tate unfavorably contrasts the plantation society of the Lower South to the "pioneer nationalism" of his own region in the Upper South. The "effete *nouveau riche*" character of the Lower South that is later transposed in Tate's fiction to Tidewater Virginia becomes the villain in *Jefferson Davis*. According to Bradbury, Tate found it increasingly necessary "to eliminate and define in his attempt to establish a tradition which [could] sustain his version of a historical, rather than a religious, heritage" (91).

Perhaps such tension between southern regions then explains the Fugitive proclamation that they were doing nothing so much as fleeing the Brahmins of the Old South. While southern nationalism forms the context for much of their work, that nationalism frequently is localized to the Upper South. Because they approached their southernness from an Upper South perspective, they helped broaden the framework of southern literature. The nineteenth century saw few examples of prominent writers from Kentucky and Tennessee. Notable exceptions are Mary Murfree and George Washington Harris, but all in all, the region saw a dearth even greater than that in the Deep South. Thus, in declaring their desire to flee "the high-caste Brahmins of the Old South," they were separating themselves from the world of the mythologized Deep South planter, not the rural landscape and yeomen of their own Upper South.

John Crowe Ransom suggests this division between the two regions in his Fugitive poem entitled "Old Mansion." The mansion, this "old house" as he describes it, does not call up visions of "monstrous chateaux on the Loire." Although, as he says, the house is of "sufficient state," it has a "beauty not for depicting by old vulgarians / Reiterations that gentle readers abhor." It has no "Towers, arcades, or forbidding fortress walls" and "no courts kept, but grave rites and funerals." A number of Ransom's other poems, among them "Janet Waking" and "Bells for John Whiteside's Daughter," celebrate a simple country life, and other poets contributed selections to *The Fugitive* about yeomen or country folk, including Warren's Alf Burt, Lytle's Edward Graves, and Davidson's Fiddler Dow and Eph Dickon, the Old Man of Thorn.

Donald Davidson's *The Tall Men* (1927) stands as one of the clearest statements that the necessity of a southern way of life was specifically connected to the Upper South. Two years after the Fugitives ceased publication of their magazine, Davidson published this book-length poem in nine parts. It depicts the earliest yeoman farmers of the Upper South, heroic men who are brave and strong, who make new homes on the frontier with their wives and families. Davidson's heroic yeomen reappear in his later poems, including those in *The Old War*. The protagonist of *The Tall Men* is a man who carries the blood of the "tall men" who settled the Upper South. He is a Tennessean who fights in World War I, lives in Nashville, and marries a woman from Ohio, just as Davidson did. The prologue, entitled "The Long Street," introduces the image that unifies the sequence. The persona walks down a long street, a street that moves chronologically from his regional past into his present in the twentieth century.

As the poem opens, the present-day Tennessean is "Pacing the long street where is no summer / But only burning summer." In his modern world, "the baked curve of asphalt, smooth, trodden, / Covers dead earth that once was quick with grass." The long street leads back through the history of Tennessee to its settlement, when tall men living on the eastern side of the Appalachian Mountains heard "a hunter's tale that rolled like wind / Across the mountains once." The persona of the poem views these men as heroic and strong, for they "talked with their rifles bluntly and sang to the hills / With a whet of axes." These tall men had grown restless in their homes on the eastern edge of the mountains, and soon they began heading westward. They brought their wives with them, "To rock the hickory cradles and to mould / Bullets for words that said: 'Give way, Red Man.'" Davidson's "tall men" sow seeds of grain and of children. They stay in this place to create new lives, to put down roots despite the pangs of hunger that force them to eat acorns, despite the night cry of the owl and the sight of a friend "furred with arrows, across his plough."

The bones of tall men now lie deep within this land, within the Tennessee earth, but their "tallness" still runs within the blood of the Tennessee people. That tallness, Davidson writes, is "not in what you eat or drink / But in the seed of man." Now in this modern age, a new generation marches off to war in Europe. In "The Faring," "Faces gather and merge and build a face / Born as mine from an ancient clay and spittle." As they cross the sea, the men huddle with their guns and packs below deck. As men from Tennessee, they carry their tallness within them, in their blood. In the ship they seem like children within the womb. They huddle in the belly, and although that tallness may be within them, it seems stunted and immature as they make their voyage. Yet in battle, they become riflemen. When they return to the United States, they return to a world of concrete slabs and rubber tires, to "stony faces, averted eyes, / Garroting [them] with sneers—." The modern world does not understand their tallness, nor can it appreciate the sacrifices they have made. Davidson points to the lingering influence of these men and their lives, as he also does in *The Tennessee* when he suggests the influence of the yeomanry on the culture of the Upper South. The true Tennesseans are those who carry a history of courage and endurance, a history born of the yeoman's struggle.

In *I'll Take My Stand*, Donald Davidson espouses a more explicit view of the divisions he saw in the South and the necessity of returning to the South's purer roots. Davidson suggests in "A Mirror for Artists" that the southern historical consciousness had too often been mistakenly defined as "merely romantic and gallant." Southern society should instead be qualified as a "fair balance of aristocratic and democratic elements." He claims for the South a "diversity within unity" that was capable of producing leaders who represented both the aristocratic and democratic elements: on the one hand, a Thomas Jefferson, and on the other an Andrew Jackson; a Robert E. Lee, and a Stonewall Jackson (53). Claiming for the South a more democratic context, Davidson also points out the potential dangers if the nation moves away from its agrarian roots. In particular, he remarks on the dangers faced by the arts if the country is industrialized. "Art in its great periods has rarely been purely aristocratic," he says (36). Because industrialization will change the character of American society, Davidson explains, the arts will suffer. He defines societies in which the arts have flourished as primarily "stable, religious, and agrarian." Industrialization will "extinguish the meaning of the arts" (29). Suggesting here, too, his interest in the folk arts, Davidson claims that the only answer is an "agrarian restoration; and that, in America, the South, past and present, furnishes a living example of an agrarian society, the preservation of which is worth the most heroic effort that men can give in a time of crisis" (30).

No one can say, though, that the agrarian life the majority of the Agrarians described was any less idealistic than that portrayed in nineteenth-century plantation novels. Despite Andrew Lytle's attempts at accuracy, his portrait of a Tennessee farmer and his family in "The Hind Tit," his contribution to *I'll Take My Stand,* is as politically manipulative as any of William Gilmore Simms's plantation scenes. Pointing out, quite rightly, that the yeomanry was the largest class of people in the South, Lytle describes in detail the life of a yeoman farmer before industrialization corrupted his way of life. This farmer lives in Rutherford County, Tennessee, around 1900. His grandfather owned roughly three to five hundred acres of land and "perhaps a slave or two in better days" (218), but unlike the planter, the yeoman's grandfather and his sons worked beside their slaves in the fields. The yeoman now owns about two hundred acres. One hundred acres are cultivated, while sixty are in woods and pasture, and forty are "waste land," land that is not suitable for cultivation but does offer some pasturage. The farmer and his family live in a dogtrot, two-story cabin that has been weatherboarded, and the dogtrot has been enclosed. To the right off the dogtrot is the main room of the house where the farmer and his wife sleep and where the youngest children sleep on pallets on the floor. Arranged in a semicircle before a large fireplace at the center of the room are handmade hickory chairs. A special chair is always held vacant for "Mammy," the farmer's "tough leather-skinned" mother, who sits in front of the fire and smokes. Dry leaf tobacco on the mantel fills the room with its strong acrid odor. The kitchen, located in the ell built off the back of the house, now houses an iron range—the open fireplace has been closed in. But the iron range, according to Lytle, has "added to the order of the establishment's life without disrupting it" (219). Meats have been cured in the smokehouse, and a large woodpile is neatly arranged close by the kitchen door.

The family rises each morning before dawn. The farmer's wife works hard in the kitchen preparing the morning meal while the boys go to the barn for the chores with their father who gives instructions for the daily activities. The girls help their mother in the kitchen or perhaps milk the cows. After the milking, the girls bring the milk to the house for churning. All this work is accomplished before breakfast is even served. After breakfast, the farmer and his sons go to the fields but not before the farmer has "consult[ed] the signs": "Lightning in the south is a sign of drought. If the moon lies on its back, it is holding water; if it is tilted so that the water can run out, the season will be dry" (224). These signs will predict how the day's work will progress. If the day is a leisurely one, the boys may go fishing. Because their father does not keep books, "their time is their own" (224–25). The family comes in from the fields at eleven o'clock for dinner. "A social event of the first importance" (226), the dinner meal is not served until the entire family arrives. The table is piled high with vegetable dishes, meats, and breads, and over the meal, the family members share stories of their morning experiences. After eating with hearty appetites, they all take a rest and then return to their duties, working in the fields or doing chores around the house. Although the family works hard during the day, by nightfall, they gather at the supper table and then on the front porch where a son might play the guitar or neighborhood boys might stop by to court one of the farmer's daughters.

Despite the harshness of the life a yeoman farmer and his family would have endured, the world of Lytle's yeomanry in "The Hind Tit" is one of purity and typical abundance. From the farmer's table that is brimming with "hot, steaming vegetables . . . a heaping plate of fried chicken, a turkey, a plate of guineas, or a one-year ham" (226) to the farmer's social engagements that range from ice-cream socials to barn dances, the life of the yeomanry that Lytle represents is clearly idealized and built on a nostalgia for a past way of life that Lytle believed was rapidly fading. In fact, though, that way of life probably never existed in the form that Lytle describes for us in his essay.

Lytle's efforts in "The Hind Tit" have much in common with the work of historian Frank Owsley. Lytle, like Owsley, believed that the yeoman had been overshadowed by the planter in southern histories and literature. Indeed, the yeoman had been marginalized, most likely because he did not possess the monetary and the political strength of the planter. The 1930s, though, saw a concerted effort, even by social scientists like Owsley, to rewrite southern history. He and a group of students at Vanderbilt took up the effort to research and redefine what they believed to be the South's true inheritance. Even the title of the first chapter of Owsley's *Plain Folk of the Old South* (1945) is telling: "Southern Society: A Reinterpretation." Explaining that "Much of the history of this great country has been written upon assumptions which have never been thoroughly tested," Owsley points specifically to the absence in the history books of a large population of rural middle-class southerners in the antebellum period. Stating that this is "perhaps, the most important assumption of them all," he says that "volumes and shelves" of histories on the antebellum period and the Civil War categorize southerners as planters, slaves, and poor whites. According to Owsley, the history books suggest that a large white middle class did not exist in the antebellum South (viii–ix). In *Plain Folk of the Old South,* Owsley attempts to prove that this assumption is incorrect.

Owsley suggests similar opinions in his essay for *I'll Take My Stand.* In "The Irrepressible Conflict," he defines the southern yeoman's past in relation to classical civilization. Southern agrarian society has classical roots, according to Owsley. It was the Romans who most shared the southerner's relationship to the earth: they were "brave, sometimes crude, but open and without guile." "They reeked of the soil, of the plow and the spade; they had wrestled with virgin soil and forests; they could build log houses and were closer to many Southerners than even the English gentleman in his moss-covered stone house" (70). Whereas the planter is typically characterized as a forebear of the English cavalier, Owsley claims for the yeoman a tradition even older. The Gracchi, Owsley explains, were "lovers of the soil," and they died attempting to restore the yeoman to that soil (71). In *I'll Take My Stand* Owsley grants that southern society might be planter class or yeomanry, "It might be crude or genteel, but it everywhere was fundamentally alike and natural" (72).

Yet in reframing the South's history within the context of the common folk (and in effect, within a context close to the democratic values upon which the United States was founded), "the irrepressible conflict, the house divided against itself" (91) becomes a different sort of conflict than the one defined by many outsiders. Owsley's argument gives substance to the view that the Civil War was fought over states' rights rather than over slavery, especially when he explains that slavery "was no essential part of the agrarian civilization in the South" and that "without slavery the economic and social life of the South would have not been radically different" (76). If, then, the South was a society based on the yeomanry, slavery would not have played a significant role because the yeoman would have owned only a few—if any—slaves. Owsley's interpretation reaffirms southern political claims of the period and softens the race issue of the Civil War.

Despite his elitist views in *I'll Take My Stand*, Ransom, looking back at the book in 1933 in his essay entitled "Happy Farmers," seems to clearly define *I'll Take My Stand* within the context of the yeomanry. Specifically identifying the agrarian economy as what he believes is "the proper economy for the American farmer," he describes agrarianism as "old-fashioned farming," a combination of subsistence farming as the main priority and "money farming" as a secondary objective. "It should be both, but in a certain order," Ransom says (527–28). Subsistence should come first, before a farmer should make money providing for others beyond his home. "The apostasy of American farmers from primary subsistence farming is the greatest disaster our country has yet suffered," he writes, "it is fortunate that it can still be undone" (530).

Labeling "the technique of subsistence on good land, with inexpensive tools" as a tradition, Ransom identifies its roots as a good deal older than the present "absolute money economy" (529). It is a tradition that provided an abundant life for generations of Americans. Ransom is careful, however, to point out that the standard of living for the old-fashioned farmer cannot be measured in monetary terms. Although the number of Americans living traditional agrarian lives has greatly decreased, Ransom explains, this tradition can still be reclaimed. Outlining what he describes as the tradition's "constituent canons," he claims for subsistence farming a life that he says leaves the farmer in little need of money: "To raise the great bulk of the foods for the family . . . to can, preserve, and cure for the winter . . .

to do plain carpentering . . . to do amateur landscape gardening . . . to work mainly with literal horse-power, mule-power, man-power; to feed all the animals, as well as the persons, from the land; to fertilize the land by the periodic use of grass crops" (529).

Ransom's plan takes into account the various facets of life on the farm; he even notes that the farm would be a pleasant environment with the farmer's able landscaping and his skill at carpentry. But if such a pleasant environment does not in itself encourage a farmer to stay on the land, Ransom also suggests other means to legislate "official encouragement" for the farmer. "Taxes, high but not quite prohibitive," he says, "might be levied against the sale of farm tractors and other specified heavy farm machinery" (533–34). He suggests that commercial fertilizers also be taxed. Ransom recognizes the benefits of unemployment relief that have put the "destitute citizen back on the land" but advocates that this citizen receive instruction on farming and periodic supervision so as to ascertain if he should be given the title to the land or be evicted from the property. These controls, Ransom says, should help lead American society back to a destiny that is "to support an excellent order of citizens, who will be economic dualists, men of universal integrity and freedom even while they perform a professional function." They will be "happy farmers," "farmers with more room, and more heart, than most of the farmers of the world" (531).

By the 1933 publication of Ransom's "Happy Farmers," there was little left of the elitist idealism originally expressed in *I'll Take My Stand*. Before he resigned from the Agrarian group, John Gould Fletcher had shifted back and forth between his original elitist ideologies and the ideal of the yeoman. Owsley's voice became a prominent one in the group, and the number of essays Davidson published far outnumbered the others'. Allen Tate joined the Distributists, a philosophical movement founded on religious principles that was critical of both socialism and capitalism, and valued a society based on independent farming and small industry. As Paul K. Conkin explains in *The Southern Agrarians*, "All the Agrarians joined in an almost populist indictment of money and privilege and joined in efforts to decentralize production, to restore productive property to as many people as possible, and to nationalize or closely regulate all remaining large firms" (170). Essays by the Agrarians filled the pages of the *American Review*, which was intended to publish the work of four groups: the Humanists, the Neo-Thomists, the Agrarians, and the Distributists. The Agrarians continued to bolster their criticism of northern industrialization, which more and more defined the North as an elitist economy that exploited Americans.

The essays published by the Agrarians after *I'll Take My Stand* were increasingly practical rather than theoretical. In his introduction to *Forty Acres and Steel Mules*, for example, Herman Clarence Nixon states that he intends in the book "a broader program of agricultural reconstruction than I read into the writings which have come from most members of [the Agrarian] group since 1930" (v). Andrew Lytle, who with Lyle Lanier was working out a plan for returning "five million" people to the land, believed that the group's next joint publication should concern itself with "the basic matters of . . . the farms and the farmers themselves" (Young 72). That next and last joint project for many of them would be *Who Owns America?*

By the time *Who Owns America?* was published, those Agrarians still active in speaking on political and social issues were firmly entrenched within the yeoman ideal. The promotional literature for the book states a clear focus on the yeoman: "This book is a rational, organized attempt to clear a path that the average reader can follow. This path leads away from both Fascism and Communism, toward a modern realization of Jeffersonian democracy; away from centralization and economic slavery, to small-scale production and the independence of property ownership" (Underwood 245). Subtitled "A New Declaration of Independence," *Who Owns America?* opens with an introduction written by Herbert Agar warning readers of the importance of preserving the American dream—"the freedom of men who do not have to be anybody's dependent, or anybody's toady" (viii). Without the realization of that dream, readers "may soon be working side by side in the concentration camps," Agar cautions (x). In "Looking Down the Cotton Row," George Marion O'Donnell, a new member of the Agrarian group, urges government assistance to small farmers and to tenant farmers so that they might *be* small farmers; the end result, he believes, would be the restoration of "liberty based on property" (177). According to O'Donnell, the yeoman farm must replace the mass production plantation of the cotton-growing industry so that a "healthy Southern agrarianism" will prevail (174). Andrew Lytle contributed an essay entitled "The Small Farm Secures the State," a celebration of the livelihood farm and similar in many ways to his contribution to *I'll Take My Stand*. In his essay, "The Foundations of Democracy," Owsley asserts the importance of private property as one of the key principles set forth by the Jeffersonians and argues for "a new Constitution" to "reconstruct the Federal Government from center to circumference." According to Thomas Underwood in his recent biography of Allen Tate, the Agrarians claimed in *Who Owns America?* that what was being "assaulted" was not a southern but an American way of life (246).

The Agrarians seemed aware, too, of the need to make their goals appear to be national ones rather than southern ones. In effect, they took up arms again, but they needed to be circumspect in addressing their audience. In a letter concerning *Who Owns America?* Tate wrote to Donald Davidson, "Our purpose is to be heard, and we can't be heard now if our program is set forth as primarily sectional. That is all there is to it. Our choice lies between a temporary disguise for our ultimate objective, in which case we can get attention, and writing avowedly sectional articles to be read chiefly by ourselves. It is my impression that this has been our conduct since 1931" (Fain and Young 293). It was a covert battle that needed to be fought, according to Tate. But the war seemed to be lost again. Ransom wrote Tate on September 17, 1936: "*Patriotism* has nearly eaten me up, and I've got to get out of it" (Young and Core 217). Not long after, Ransom wrote again to Tate, saying that he was "signing off" from agrarianism "but a little by degrees." After a move to Kenyon College in Ohio, Ransom wrote Edwin Mims on June 8, 1937: "I have about contributed all I have to [the regionalist or agrarian] movements, and I have of late gone almost entirely into pure literary work" (Young and Core 223).

Actually living the "agrarian experiment" also became unrealistic, despite the efforts of some of the Agrarians. Allen Tate and his wife Caroline Gordon had hoped to live the agrarian experiment at a home in Clarksville, Tennessee, that Tate's brother Ben purchased for them. Named Benfolly, because of Ben's folly with the purchase, Tate and Gordon's agrarian life there also became folly. Gordon wrote to her friend Sally Wood, "I love to have space around me, and I love to dig in the dirt and walk in the woods." But Tate soon found such agrarian living not as much to his liking as he had believed it would be. He offered to do the dishes if Gordon would hoe in the garden. Gordon wrote to Wood, "He has the strangest attitude toward the country— the same appreciation you'd have for a good set in the theatre. I think Allen feels toward Nature as I do toward mathematics—respectful indifference. He walks over the garden hailing each tomato and melon with amazement—and never sees any connection between planting seeds and eating fruit" (Makowsky 69). Not long after they moved into Benfolly, Allen Tate hired a local farmer named Jesse Rye to raise small crops, such as watermelons and cantaloupe, on the property. Rye's wife said in a 1991 interview that her husband was hired because "Mr. Allen" was unable to farm himself. According to Mrs. Rye, Tate would watch her husband as he farmed. "I don't think Mr. Allen knew anything about farming," she said. Gordon wasn't any more successful at agrarian living than was her husband, but it was a matter of finishing household duties and making time for writing—not her lack of interest—that left her little time for gardening. She soon found herself so busy at the house just seeing to housekeeping chores for her family and their many guests that she often complained in her letters to Sally Wood of having little time to write. If indeed the Tates had truly desired to attempt an agrarian experiment at Benfolly, their methods thus seem curious ones.

Lytle seems to have been the one able to achieve the most success in living an agrarian life and creating a body of literature intimately tied to that way of life. From stories like "Mr. McGregor" and novels including *The Velvet Horn* (1957), the South's yeoman appears again and again in Lytle's writings. Lytle's life, too, was led as one very much tied to his family property and to his agrarian roots. Nevertheless, his novel *A Name for Evil* (1947), generally regarded as a retelling of Henry James's *The Turn of the Screw*, tells of Henry Brent's attempts to reclaim his family farm and the resulting insanity that overcomes him and brings about his ruin. Obsessed with the life of his ancestor, Major Brent, Henry possesses a dream of an Eden that one literary scholar describes as "too private even for an Eve" (Bradford, "The Passion of Craft," 382).

While Lytle idealized the yeoman farmer, gave this figure a prominent place in his fiction, and even tried to live as one himself, Robert Penn Warren took from his experience in the Agrarian movement what he has called "the broad general idea of man's place in nature." Although Warren's agrarianism was grounded in the Jeffersonian image of the yeoman farmer, he also recognized the impossibilities of leading such a life. "You couldn't build a society on it, but you could take up a lot of slack," he once said (Warren, "Talk with Warren," 230–31). Perhaps the Agrarian movement—and the figure of the yeoman in particular—had a more subtle influence on Warren's work. Not the yeoman tradition itself but perhaps the Americanness of it could be said to have prompted Warren to explore American issues and America's historical roots in *Democracy and Poetry, The Legacy of the Civil War,* and *Brother to Dragons.* Warren's view is decidedly toward an American Democracy—with its triumphs and its failures and shortcomings. In *Brother to Dragons,* for example, Warren tackles the issue of slavery not solely in a southern context but as part of a larger portrait of the hopes of our nation's founding fathers for their budding democracy, examining the question within the framework of Jefferson's desire for an agrarian society. As our country's first poet laureate, Warren could speak for all of us, not just for the South.

Later generations of writers, including Peter Taylor and Madison Smartt Bell, have written of agrarianism's influence on their works. Bell sees his fictional work as expanding on that of the Agrarians, and he has been greatly influenced by and interested in their "sense of something gone radically wrong" in the world. According to Bell in a 1992 interview, the question at the focus of contemporary life is "is it possible to commit species suicide?" "That is the southern question in a broader form," one that informs and shapes the focus of Bell's own fiction. "The Agrarians didn't know that's what they were looking at when they predicted the kinds of disasters that would come about as the result of hegemony of an industrial society over an agrarian society," Bell has said, "but their sense of danger had a lot to do with where we're at now" ("An Interview," 11).

That sense of danger suggests the continuing awareness among writers like Bell that the agrarian values of the yeoman South continue to have pertinence, continue to shape the South as it moves into the future. The prospect of doing something about the South and its history, as Tate wrote to Ransom, became the important task of doing something about America and its future.

3 "The Dawn of Direct and Unafraid Creation"

JEAN TOOMER AND HIS *CANE*

The impetus for the creation of Jean Toomer's *Cane* came from a two-month trip Toomer made to the South in 1921. Then living in Washington, DC, Toomer had accepted a position as substitute principal of the Sparta Agricultural and Industrial Institute, an all-black school in Georgia, the home state of his father and grandfather. In making the trip south, Toomer not only traveled to his familial place but also made a journey of self-discovery, a journey into his racial past. Writing after his return to Washington, Toomer explained in a letter to *The Liberator* magazine that the trip was "the starting point of almost everything of worth that I have done." There in Georgia, he wrote, "I heard folk-songs come from the lips of Negro peasants. I saw the rich dusk beauty that I had heard many false accounts about, and of which til then, I was somewhat skeptical. And a deep part of my nature, a part that I had repressed, sprang suddenly to life and responded to them . . . My point of view has not changed; it has deepened; it has widened" (D. Turner 128–29).

Toomer is said to have begun writing *Cane* as he traveled back north on the train. In retrospect, he claimed that in Georgia he had for the first time seen the African American "not as a ps[eu]do-urbanized and vulgarized, a semi-Americanized product." He suggests here in his language that in seeing the African American "strong with the tang of fields and soil," he has now seen the African American as the true American (Benson and Dillard 28). Describing African American folk songs as "spontaneous and native utterances," Toomer wrote to Waldo Frank that this was the first time he had heard them "rolling up the valley at twilight." They were songs that filled him with "gold, and tints of an eternal purple" (Scruggs and VanDemarr 236n). Toomer also recognized his own relationship to this culture: "I had never before lived in the midst of a people gathered together by a group spirit. . . . And what I saw and felt and shared entered me, so that my people-life was uncased from the rest of myself" (McKay 8). His creative spirit was reinvigorated and redefined, he wrote to Sherwood Anderson: "My seed was planted in the cane- and cotton-fields, and in the souls of the black and white people in the small southern town. My seed was planted in *myself* down there" (D. Turner 148).

In *Cane* Toomer weaves together the story of his own personal struggle with his racial identity and his hopes for the United States. Toomer often rejected his black heritage, instead embracing his Americanness. In some ways, however, his personal struggles were motivated as much by economics as by race. Descended from a well-to-do southern family (he was the grandson of P.B.S. Pinchback who served as acting governor of Louisiana during Reconstruction), Toomer received an agricultural degree in college and was essentially a child of privilege. He saw himself as living "equally amid" the black and white races, "now white, now colored." But he emphasized that most importantly he saw himself as "naturally and inevitably an American." He claimed to know of at least seven "blood mixtures" that ran through his veins: French, Dutch, Welsh, Negro, German, Jewish, and Indian. And as a result of this mix, he believed his place in America to be "a curious one." He endeavored, he said, for a "spiritual fusion"—an intermingling of the races within himself. "Without denying a single element in me, with no desire to subdue one to the other," Toomer wrote, "I have sought to let them function as complements. I have tried to let them live in harmony" (Bontemps 21).

Toomer's interest in expressing the significance of this spiritual fusion is a primary concern in *Cane,* but it also appears in other of his writings, most significantly the poem "The Blue Meridian." When he wrote of his trip to Georgia and of the folk songs that he heard fill the southern air, he saw himself as filled with gold and "hints of eternal purple." Likewise, the color purple became for him in his writings a symbol of the American ideal—a coming together in a melting pot. In "The Blue Meridian," for example, Toomer points to this unique American inheritance of the possibility of racial integration and celebration:

Black is black, white is white,
East is east, west is west,
Is truth for the mind of contrasts;
But here the high way of the third,
The man of blue or purple.

He hoped in "Blue Meridian" to suggest the ideal—an American who is neither white nor black. Toomer also uses the purple of the sugar cane in *Cane* to signify his own attempts to come to terms with his southern black heritage as a part of himself. The sugar cane of the book's title, as a symbol of rural life, implies both the pleasures and the sufferings of living close to the southern earth. *Cane* is typically read as an individual's physical and spiritual quest for answers concerning his place within America and within humanity as a whole. It is, ultimately, a story of self-discovery and of self-definition. In *Cane*, Kabnis, like Toomer, attempts to come to terms with and to accept the truths of his racial past and ultimately to redefine himself within the framework of that past. In fact, Toomer once wrote to Waldo Frank that "Kabnis is Me" (McKay 9). Kabnis sees both the beauty of his connections to the southern earth and to the African American people, as well as the horrors of the African American past in slavery. Ultimately, though, Kabnis must reabsorb those truths in order to recognize himself as African American. It is through the southern folk's relationship to the southern soil—a soil that produces the harvested cane—that both Kabnis and Toomer recognize and celebrate their African American past.

Toomer's portrait of rural life thus revolves around the figures of the common man and woman living close to the southern earth. While some of the Georgia blacks of the book work in the mills, they remain close to the southern soil. They have remained in an agricultural community rather than moving to Chicago, Washington, or other places set off from the earth by slabs of concrete and automobiles. These African Americans work in the cane fields, in the mill, in their homes and serve as figures meant to emphasize the significant relationship between the African American and the rural past of the South. In many ways, then, the book explores the relationship between southernness and Americanness. Toomer identified himself first of all as an American, but in writing *Cane* he also worked to come to terms with his southern roots. He believed, too, in the importance for American society of facing the facts of the southern past and then moving on.

Toomer's representation of the rural South as a pastoral setting and as a sort of salvation can be troubling, however. Why, in the first place, did Toomer choose to write a text in which, as Lucinda MacKethan claims, he "approaches a kind of hysterical rapture as he displays the vitality of the 'song-lit' race of blacks and the Southland they inhabit" (232). The shape of *Cane,* according to MacKethan, is implicitly tied to the African American's place in the modern world. The book is, accordingly, "a version of Southern pastoral perceived with the black man's double vision of deep belonging and forced alienation" (231). The intensity of Toomer's emotional representation of the rural South—the "hysterical rapture" with which he writes—seems then the result of the anguish he felt (and that Kabnis feels) in being pulled two directions, both toward and away from a region that gave shape to his identity.

As a pastoral, *Cane* is structured around the contrast between urban life in Washington and Chicago and the rural life of Georgia. The book's first section, set in the rural South, calls up images of African American folk living close to the earth, working the fields, and recognizing and enjoying the natural elements that surround them. Toomer writes not only of the beauty of Georgia sunsets but also of the harsh realities country folk face. Natural elements such as fields of cotton, corn, and cane; the moon; pine trees; and the soil play prominent roles in this section. The second section of the book is filled with streets and alleys, apartment buildings, theaters and box seats, cars, dance clubs, and bars. Toomer suggests the vitality that the African American brings to an urban setting like Washington, but he also describes the cities—especially Chicago—as unnatural and artificial. In many ways, *Cane* is a pastoral work in a very modern and in a very southern sense. Toomer recognized that his book represented the passing of a way of life that was impossible in the modern world. "Back to nature," Toomer said, "even if desirable, was no longer possible, because industry had taken nature into itself" (Helbling 98–99). Toomer describes the folk-spirit as "walking in to die on the modern desert." Claiming a beauty for that spirit, suggesting its death was tragic, Toomer recollected, "Just this seemed to sum life for me. And this was the feeling I put into 'Cane.' Cane was a swan-song. It was a song of an end" (Wintz 77).

As a swan-song, *Cane* has a good deal in common with other writings of the Southern Literary Renaissance. Toomer deals with issues of identity, an escape from the South and a return in recognition of the significance of the past and its influence on the future, and the essential—but conflicted—ties of the southerner to the southern land. Bernard Bell describes the rural African American of *Cane* as an "admirable, primitive, intensely human being—liberated by his kinship with the earth, uninhibited, free, responsive to the soil and the sun, mingling the glories of two cultures, and expressing his soul in native wisdom, in the joyful and sad songs of work and love and religion" (109). In the book, Toomer suggests that although the atrocities of slavery should not be forgotten, the modern African American must recognize his or her relationship to the southern soil in order to fully know self. He sees the life of the rural folk as positive and fulfilling, a part of himself that he must also recognize and celebrate. Toomer wanted to write of the strength and endurance of African Americans of the rural South and to preserve in writing a rural life that he recognized was rapidly fading in the twentieth century.

Cane continues to be identified as Toomer's greatest literary achievement. His trip to the rural South ultimately became his most powerful literary inspiration. He recognized, too, the importance of writing the southern black back into American literary history, not as a planter's slave but as his true self. In "The Negro Emergent," Toomer writes "that in proportion as [the African American] discovers what is real within him, he will create, and by that act at once create himself and contribute his value to America" (54). Not only fulfilling Toomer's need for a creative outlet, the trip and the resulting book became his way to tell about the South, to tell the truths of the region. He also believed that *Cane* helped to preserve folk life in the South, including the folk songs and the African American church, before it was destroyed by industrialization. Toomer hoped to encourage other African American writers to write about those truths and thus to discover what was real within themselves.

Shaping his book within the pastoral tradition, Toomer incorporates and celebrates folk songs of the rural people as symbolic of the resiliency and spiritual strength of southern blacks. Even more significantly, however, he strove to write of "a new order" of man, the emergence of an American people garnered with an ability not just to survive but also to endure and to prevail. In his 1931 "A New Race in America" he states explicitly that he himself "proclaims" this new ideal: "Now is the time of the birth of a new order, a new vision, a new ideal of man" (Rusch 105).

Many of the images in the first section of *Cane* illustrate ways that a shared racial spirit has carried southern blacks through times of cultural devastation and loss. Like the black harvesters in the poem "Reapers" who are unfeeling to the "startled, squealing" field rat run over by the mower as the workers clear the field, the human spirit is often ignored rather than cherished. Even though the blade is blood-stained, the workers continue their work, paying no attention to the rat's suffering. Likewise, in "Karintha," the men do not recognize that Karintha's soul is "a growing thing ripened too soon" (4). The piece expresses the strength of the human spirit and the inability of many to recognize its value. Another piece, entitled "Becky," suggests once again the human loss that results from prejudices. Its theme of racial identity confusion is frequently addressed throughout the book and certain to have been influenced by Toomer's own life. Becky, a white woman with two black sons, lives in a house by the railroad tracks. The persona of the poem and his friend travel on a train by the house, which has crumbled into ruin. No one knows if Becky's body is in the ruins—and, indeed, no one really seems to care except that Becky now is an apparition that is the subject of folk stories. Even religion offers little hope as a Bible lying upon the house's ruins "flaps its leaves with an aimless rustle on her mound" (9).

By contrast, other selections from the first section of *Cane* suggest the possibilities that come from a connection to the earth. In "November Cotton Flower," for example, the southern landscape is approaching wintertime:

> Boll-weevil's coming, and the winter's cold,
> Made cotton-stalks look rusty, seasons old,
> And cotton, scarce as any southern snow,
> Was vanishing; . . .

The earth and its animals fight for survival. The soil is described as "drouth fighting," and it drains the streams to find nourishment. The birds have searched for water deep in the wells cut into the earth, and now the wells are full of the carcasses of those birds that sought refuge from the harsh environment. Although the southern landscape at first appears deep in despair, a flower blooms, suggesting the possibilities of renewal.

Another group of pieces in this first section of *Cane* focuses not only on the importance and the power of personal expression but also on the necessity of the southern black's desire and determination to achieve self-expression. In "Carma," for example, the persona is part of the poem. As Charles Scruggs and Lee VanDemarr have said of "Carma," "There is a point of connection" in the story, "a mutual 'gaze' the narrator reads as sexual but which also links storyteller and protagonist, as if that 'gaze'—the recognition that is both sexual and transsexual—implies that the narrator bears a responsibility to tell her tale: if he does not do so, only the *Ishmaelite* will" (148). In the line "Time and space have no meaning in a canefield," Toomer suggests that the cane field is a realm in which the African American can find equality and peace. But the African American faces some responsibility as well, as the narrator indicates in "Cotton Song" when he adds, "Cant blame God if we don't roll." The tale must be born; the tale must be told. The potential and the strength of the southern black spirit and culture suggest the possibilities of a New Negro, a "new vision of his race" in the poem "Song of the Son." That "new vision" should be celebrated in verse: "Pour O pour that parting soul in song." But time is passing, and soon it may be too late:

> In time, for though the sun is setting on
> A song-lit race of slaves, it has not set;
> Though late, O soil, it is not too late yet
> To catch thy plaintive soul, leaving, soon gone,
> Leaving, to catch thy plaintive soul soon gone. (14)

The cane and the pine celebrate this new vision in "Georgia Dusk." As men who hold "race memories" of "king and caravan, / High-priests, an ostrich, and a juju-man" singing as they follow a footpath through the swamp, it is as if "the chorus of the cane / Is caroling a vesper to the stars . . . Above the sacred whisper of the pines" (15).

Despite this vision of promise and significance in the African American's creative expression, the narrator of *Cane* still cannot recognize the part of himself that is southern, as represented in the eponymous "Fern." The narrator sees the South in Fern's face: "the whole countryside seemed to flow into her eyes" (17). Yet he is unable to merge with her, make love to her, stay with her. At this point in *Cane,* the narrator (like Toomer himself) has not been able to incorporate into his being the place that will ultimately become his creative inspiration—that is, the South. The African American, according to Toomer, faces both self-imposed and external circumstances that do not allow him to recognize his heritage and to confirm the importance of his being. In "Esther," for example, Esther's mulatto father is a storeowner who uses his race only to make money in the black community. The family's ideals are clearly white middle-class, and Esther's family members are essentially outsiders to the black community. Two other selections, "Conversion" and "Portrait in Georgia," point out that religion has been used in the United States to force assimilation upon African Americans. Christianity, Toomer suggests, has been instrumental in suppressing African Americans.

This first section of the book closes with "Blood-Burning Moon," the story of a black woman who is courted by two men—one white and one black. The story sums up the potential for a new age for the African American, but it also points to what African Americans must struggle against. The chapter reflects, too, the violence that can come from southern society's determination to draw lines between the races. The blood-burning moon of the title rises above the prewar cotton factory to suggest the horrific past African Americans have faced in the South. The factory's floorboards may be rotting, but the hand-hewn oak beams are still solid. Probably crafted by slaves, the beams suggest the societal framework that still remains in the South, a remainder and a reminder of the prejudices and atrocities of the past. Although the South seems in the process of change into a new South, still the past lingers on.

The two men in the story, Bob Stone and Tom Burwell, desire Louisa and love her. Bob is the son of the white family that employs her, and Tom, known in the community as Big Boy, works in the fields and hopes to own his own farm some day. Tom has proposed marriage to her, but she plans to meet Bob later in the canebrake. Louisa cannot decide between the two men. She wants them both, but neither man can accept that fact. For Tom, she represents a settled life on the earth he hopes to farm. For Bob, she is an enigma. He takes her as a master would have taken his slave in the olden days, but since the end of the Civil War his family has, as the narrator says, "lost ground." But he remains attracted to her: "it was because she was nigger that he went to her. Sweet . . . The scent of boiling cane came to him" (34). Seeing Louisa with Tom, Bob lunges at him. A fight ensues, with Bob drawing a knife. Bob is stabbed, but he makes it back to "white town" to say that Tom is the one who stabbed him. A mob captures Tom and drags him to the factory where he is burned alive. Louisa's inability to decide between the two men represents the conflict at the heart of *Cane*. She struggles with a conflicted identity, a desire to encompass all when that possibility is not yet open to her.

"The gray crimson-splashed beauty of the dawn," according to Toomer, will not usher in a positive future unless southern blacks realize the importance of recognizing their roots in the rural South. Over and over again in *Cane*, Toomer portrays the South as an uneducated rural woman with whom the persona (an educated man) should join, but for much of the book the persona rejects that union. In "Avey," a prose piece from the second section of *Cane*, set in the city, the narrator sees the South as an "orphan-woman." He believes he knows her: "Avey and my real relation to her, I thought I came to know" (47). But still he does not absorb her into his being. He is at once drawn to her and repelled by her. He calls her lazy, but he is attracted to her.

While Toomer wrote to Waldo Frank in 1922 saying that he was "nostalgic for the streets and faces of Washington" (Rusch 13), Toomer believed that urbanization can isolate human beings from one another and leave the human being in spiritual decline. The second section of *Cane* focuses on this dehumanizing effect. In the poem "Beehive," the persona is among a swarm of a million bees. He is "getting drunk with silver honey," but he wishes he "might fly out past the moon / and curl forever in some far-off farmyard." It is that far-off farmyard that in the city seems so distant. Characters like the unnamed urban woman in "Calling Jesus" also find themselves lost. The persona describes the woman's soul as being "like a little thrust-tailed dog that follows her, whimpering" (58).

A similar type of character is Dorris in "Theater." John, the manager's brother, watches the dance girls as they practice. He looks at the girls individually, trying to "trace origins and plot destinies" (52). As the girls dance and sing, the men clap and the walls of the theater sing and push inward, pressing John toward "a center of physical ecstasy" (53). Dorris is attracted to John, but she is obsessed with the differences between them. "Aint I as good as him? Couldnt I have got an education if I'd wanted one? Dont I know respectable folks, lots of em, in Philadelphia and New York and Chicago? Aint I had men as good as him?" Dorris asks (53–54). "Hell, he cant love. He's too skinny. His lips are too skinny. He wouldnt love me anyway, only for that" (54–55). Dorris is, significantly, described as wearing purple stockings. The purple coloring of these beautiful legs that John "feels" with his eyes, these legs that he desires, represents Dorris's clear connection to the South. Her sexuality is linked to the southern earth, for her "Glorious songs are the muscles of her limbs. And her singing is of canebrake loves and mangrove feastings." In John's dream, likewise, "Her face is tinted like the autumn alley. Of old flowers, or of a southern canefield, her perfume." John's heart seems to beat "tensely against her dancing body" as the walls of the theater "press his mind within her heart." But suddenly, "the shaft of light goes out the window high above him," and John's face is shadowed (55). Dorris hopes to see the influence of her dance in his face, but all she sees there is "a dead thing in the shadow which is his dream" (56). Neither will act because of what they both perceive to be the difference that separates them rather than what binds them.

One of the last selections included in the second section of *Cane* is "Box Seat," which has been described as echoing T. S. Eliot's "The Waste Land." Although the historical roots of the southern black, according to the book's narrator, may seem to suggest only hopelessness and despair, in *Cane* there remains a potential that is much more vital and real than the life force in Eliot's poem. "Shake your curled wool-blossoms . . . Open your liver lips to the lean, white spring. Stir the root-life of a withered people," Toomer says in "Box Seat," "Call them from their houses, and teach them to dream" (59). The central figure of "Box Seat" is Dan Moore, who was born in a canefield and who comes now to heal an ailing world. He calls on Muriel, who lives in one of the houses of "withered people," but she tells him that the town will not allow her to love him. She has not faced "whats real" in her life. At the Lincoln theater, the seats are bolted to the floor and the audience—the "bolted" masses (64)—watch dwarfs who box. Mr. Barry offers Muriel a rose, but she shies away. Despite her reluctance to love Moore, the potential for that love glimmers in her face as the color purple. The two poems that follow "Box Seat" and precede "Bona and Paul" suggest a desire for healing, for connecting with others who are likewise suffering. In "Prayer," the persona, when he speaks of his body and his mind as "opaque to the soul," suggests a desire for healing. In "Harvest Song," the persona of the poem has finished harvesting his oats, but now he is too cold and tired to bind them. Despite the poem's title, the persona is hungry and his throat is dry. He is "a blind man who stares across the hills, seeking stak'd fields of other harvesters." He struggles to hear the voices of the other harvesters, but he is deaf. There is a need for healing that will come from a connection to the land, Toomer suggests.

The second section of the book closes with "Bona and Paul," a chapter set in Chicago, a city that represents freedom from racial social codes. Chicago is supposedly free from the societal restrictions that dominate in southern cities, a place that offers freedom and suggests opportunities for change. Paul, an African American, is attracted to Bona, a young white woman. Bona is attracted to Paul, and she connects him specifically with images of the southern earth: "He is a candle that dances in a grove swung with pale balloons . . . He is a harvest moon. He is an autumn leaf." But he is also a "nigger." "Dont all the dorm girls say so?" she asks herself (72). She fears crossing the line between the races. The basketball game described in the first section of "Bona and Paul" is a freeing moment. Both men and women, black and white can play. There is equality in the sense that each individual is allowed to excel as each can, and there is physical contact between black and white. Ultimately, that contact results in a stirring of physical attractions between Bona and Paul.

In Chicago, Paul is accepted as a student, but his race continues to define him. His room has two windows, suggesting the dilemma that he faces. Looking out one window he envisions "a pine-matted hillock in Georgia" and "the slanting roofs of gray unpainted cabins tinted lavender." He sees an African American woman who "chants a lullaby beneath the mate-eyes of a southern planter. Her breasts are ample for the suckling of a song." As she "weans" her song, she "sends it, curiously weaving, among lush melodies of cane and corn." From the other window, in Chicago, where "a fresh stench is just arising" from the stockyards, Paul can follow the sun into himself (73).

When Bona and Paul visit a nightclub called Crimson Gardens, patrons of the club whisper questions about Paul: "What is he, a Spaniard, an Indian, an Italian, a Mexican, a Hindu, or a Japanese?" Recognizing that what people see in him is "difference"—"not attractiveness"—he sees himself "cloudy, but real" (76–77). Tonight, he believes, Bona will come to know him. When they dance, the passions rise between them: "The dance takes blood from their minds and packs it, tingling, in the torsos of their swaying bodies." As the "passionate blood leaps back into their eyes . . . they are a dizzy blood clot on a gyrating floor. They know that the pink-faced people have no part in what they feel" (79). Their passions overcoming them, they leave the club, passing by the black doorman. Something extraordinary happens to Paul. He seems to see Crimson Gardens from a distance, and it is shaded in the color purple for him. In the midst of this color is the face of the doorman, whose face "leers" and "smiles sweetly like a child's" (79). Although the leer on the doorman's face suggests he believes the outcome of the evening for Bona and Paul will be a sexual coupling, a moment of passion, Paul leaves Bona outside the club to return to the doorman to tell him, "Brother, youre wrong . . . Something beautiful is going to happen . . . the Gardens were purple like a bed of roses would be at dusk. I came back to tell you, brother, that white faces are petals of roses. That dark faces are petals of dusk. That I am going out and gather petals. That I am going out and know her whom I brought here with me to these Gardens which are purple like a bed of roses would be at dusk" (80). The men shake hands, and Paul returns to Bona, but she is gone.

Toomer wrote in a letter to Georgia O'Keefe in January 1924 that in "Bona and Paul," Paul "resolves these contrasts" between black and white "to a unity" (Rusch 281). Although Bona leaves the Gardens without Paul, Paul has envisioned the color purple, which suggests that finally he has integrated the two races within himself. Toomer now seems ready to move on to the final section of the book entitled "Kabnis," where Kabnis must go down into the depths of the southern past of slavery before "the sun arises from its cradle" (117) in the final paragraph of the book. Chicago may appear to be a modern city of promise and renewal as the name of the Gardens suggests, but ultimately the author and his character Kabnis must return to the rural South on a journey of self-awareness and understanding. They must both return to the place of familial roots in search of a usable past.

Each of the three sections of *Cane* is preceded by a prefatory page printed with a geometrical shape. The shape prefacing the first section looks like a tilted crescent moon, while the shape included at the opening of the second section looks like a dome. The final section of the book, the "Kabnis" section, is prefaced by two curves that are approaching the shape of a circle. At the opening of this final section, the circle is not complete because there is not yet unity and fulfillment in the persona's search. Toomer speaks of the completion of this circle in a letter he wrote to Waldo Frank on December 12,

1922: "From three angles, CANE's design is a circle. Aesthetically, from simple forms to complex ones, and back to simple forms. Regionally, from the South up into the North, and back into the South again. Or, from the North down into the South, and then a return North. From the point of view of the spiritual entity behind the work, the curve really starts with Bona and Paul (awakening), plunges into Kabnis, emerges in Karintha etc. swings upward into Theatre and Box Seat, and ends (pauses) in Harvest Song" (152). Kabnis returns to the South in an active attempt to reunite with it. But before he can reach that unity, he must first go down into the cellar of Father John, the old man whom the character Lewis describes as "symbol, flesh, and spirit of the past" (108). Bound within this section of the book are both images of death and of rebirth, but only by going below, into the fire of the blacksmith's shop and then into the cellar, can Kabnis finally emerge to sing his song. Significantly, too, he must go down into the earth, into the cellar, before he is reborn.

Kabnis seems both haunted and overwhelmed by the African American past of slavery and the prejudices of white society. "Night winds in Georgia are vagrant poets, whispering" and they sing,

White-man's land.
Niggers, sing.
Burn, bear black children
Till poor rivers bring
Rest, and sweet glory
In Camp Ground. (83)

Kabnis lets the book he is reading drop from his hands as he tries to go to sleep, but he does so against his will as he listens to the night winds' song. He wants to be able to sing for the South, his "songs being the lips of its soul." If he could "become the face of the South"—if he could face the South and its face could become not his fear and weakness but his strength, then he could sing for the South, for its soul. But initially he feels only despair at his efforts. "Soul. Soul hell. There aint no such thing." He is frightened by the noises of the darkness around him, in what he calls a "God-forsaken hole" (84). Even a chicken scares him and he violently wrings its neck.

Kabnis is drawn to yet repelled by the South. He prays, "Dear Jesus, do not chain me to myself and set these hills and valleys, heaving with folk-songs, so close to me that I cannot reach them." He recognizes that "radiant beauty in the night that touches and . . . tortures" him. But how can there be beauty in "Hog pens and chicken yards. Dirty red mud. Stinking outhouse"? He wonders how he could have been such a "damn fool" when he is repulsed by what he sees around him. He also concludes, "Whats beauty anyway but ugliness if it hurts you?" (85). Kabnis is described as "a promise of a soil-soaked beauty; uprooted, thinning out" (98). He is so close to the southern soil that will renew him, but he does not recognize this fact. He sees only the ugliness around him.

Even Augusta, Georgia, seems so far away from the rural world that surrounds him. Kabnis feels completely isolated from all that he believes he is. Although he might have "halfway despised" many people in Washington, now he remembers only quiet, serene streets. New York seems "a fiction" of which he had only dreamed (86). As he thinks of the city he has left behind, "an impotent nostalgia grips him. It becomes intolerable." He makes himself think about the blacks who live in a cabin nearby. "Silhouetted on a knoll about a mile away," the cabin and the life lived there suggest peace. The African Americans who live there seem comfortable and satisfied with their lives as they "farm . . . sing . . . love . . . sleep." "Things are so immediate in Georgia," he thinks to himself, as he "wonders if perhaps they can feel him. If perhaps he gives them bad dreams" (86).

Kabnis believes he has found refuge with friends he has made in the community as he and Layman eat dinner at Halsey's home. Although Kabnis identifies himself as a northern black, the "red mud" of Georgia has him trapped—at once drawn to the South but also struggling against it. Kabnis tries to talk himself into believing there is something positive about this place when he says that blacks—especially those with money—would not stay in the South if conditions were too harsh. When Kabnis points to his own family ties to the South, Halsey reminds him, "kindly remember youre in th land of cotton—hell of a land. Th white folks get th boll; th niggers get th stalk. An dont you dare touch th boll, or even look at it. They'll swing y sho"

(89). Halsey and Layman also tell Kabnis of the horrific murders of Mame Lamkins and of her child, who was cut from her womb as Mame lay lifeless in the street of the town. Her only crime, they say, was trying to hide her husband from the whites who killed her. When, suddenly, in the midst of their talk, a stone with a piece of paper wrapped around it reading "You northern nigger, its time fer y t leave. Git along now" is thrown through the window of Halsey's home, Kabnis believes the threat must be for him, and he flees from the room (92).

Kabnis has come to the South with preconceived notions about its prevalent violence toward African Americans; the story of Mame Lamkins's murder only seems to confirm his fears. But Kabnis misreads the situation because he is the outsider who wants to be the face of the South, to write about it, but still does not know it. Halsey tells Kabnis, "Nobody's after y. . . . These aint th days of hounds an Uncle Tom's Cabin, feller. White folks aint in fer all them theatrics these days. Theys more direct than that. If what they wanted was t get y, theyd have just marched right in an took y where y sat" (94). The shots Kabnis had heard were actually fired by someone hunting rabbits and possums.

There are those who act as his guides in this unfamiliar territory. Lewis, for example, is described as "what a stronger Kabnis might have been," and "in an odd faint way [he] resembles him" (97). Lewis is a northerner, who, like Kabnis, has come to the South "on a contract." When Lewis looks at Carrie, his eyes are described as "Christ-eyes" (103). Lucinda MacKethan describes Lewis as a "Savior figure" in a religion of "confrontation." According to MacKethan, when Lewis says to Kabnis, "Can't hold them, can you? Master; slave. Soil; and the overarching heavens. Dusk; dawn. They fight and bastardize you," Lewis identifies the central difficulty for an African American living in the South. On the one hand, the southern black has an essential need to feel connected to the land of the South—the land of his forebears—in order to define himself regionally and racially. But on the other hand, he must move beyond and leave behind that land associated with the atrocities of slavery and the hardships of southern blacks (235).

When Hanby, the principal of the school, fires Kabnis because he is drinking in his quarters, Halsey gives him a job at his wagon shop.

Halsey has a blacksmith working for him, and in the cellar below the shop are rooms that Halsey uses to entertain the locals. The rooms also house an elderly man who represents the past of African Americans in slavery. The elderly man—"Father John" they call him—is described by Lewis as a "mute John the Baptist of a new religion—or a tongue-tied shadow of an old" (106), for Lewis seems to recognize the relationship between the past and the present and the influence of the past and the present on the future. Kabnis wants to understand the South and know it as he believes Lewis does. Clearly, the shop and its occupant Father John carry with them symbolism of the southern past of African Americans. The cellar is a place that Kabnis associates with where "they used t stow away th worn-out, no-count [slaves]" (114). But here there is also life that comes from death, from a past associated with a deaf and blind old man. Early in the book the dead child buried under sawdust in "Karintha" and the ruins of Becky's house that might hide her corpse in "Becky" show death buried in the earth, death that sees no renewal and rebirth. But in "Kabnis," there is a sense of renewal after Kabnis goes into the cellar, into the southern earth.

The cellar is also significant because in going down into the earth, Kabnis achieves an insight that gives him the ability to write, to create. He is shaped by this experience. Halsey uses the cellar to entertain, and the women who go there with the men are prostitutes. The cellar should be read, however, as a place connected with a letting go of human emotions. By allowing himself to be open, to be a sort of conduit, Kabnis can feel the South and come face to face with it, merge with it as the author's various personas have been unable to do so in earlier sections of the book. When Lewis asks, "An artist in your way, arent you, Halsey?" (101), his words ring true to what is happening to Kabnis. Halsey is an artist as his cellar reshapes Kabnis, births him again.

Lewis describes the old man in the cellar as "symbol, flesh, and spirit of the past" (108). But Kabnis still is not able to accept that past as his own. Lewis knowingly recounts a history for Father John, saying that he was a slave taught to read the Bible by his Christian mistress who became a preacher after seeing Jesus in the rice fields.

He calls the old man a "Dead blind father of a muted folk who feel their way upward to a life that crushes or absorbs them" (106). Noting the old man's blindness, Lewis compels him to speak—an act that will be important to Kabnis in recognizing the truth that the old man holds. All Kabnis can say in response to Lewis's characterization of the old man are words of isolation and disconnection: "He aint my past," Kabnis says, "My ancestors were Southern blue-bloods." When Lewis adds, "And black," Kabnis can only reply, "Aint much difference between blue an black" (108). But Lewis recognizes that Kabnis still cannot accept his familial and racial pasts.

Carrie, too, has significance to the Kabnis section of *Cane*. Carrie has been described as representing the African American spirit and the African American's attachment to the soil and to the "primitive past" (MacKethan 236). Lewis is impulsively drawn to her, but in her he also sees "the nascent woman, her flesh already stiffening to cartilage, drying to bone. Her spirit-bloom, even now touched sullen, bitter. Her rich beauty fading." Like Carrie, the African American's spirit is fading. Lewis has an urge to reach out his hands to take Carrie's, and he does. He feels the warmth and the life of her through his palms, and her eyes are like a sunburst that "floods up and haloes him." His "Christ-eyes" look at her, and "fearlessly she loves into them." But then Carrie's face pales and she pulls away: "The sin-bogies of respectable southern colored folks clamor at her: 'Look out! Be a *good* girl. A *good* girl. Look out!'" (103). She struggles to find her basket that is now on the floor and systematically returns to her duty of feeding the old man.

Lewis wants Carrie to go north with him, as Toomer will return north to write about his new connection to the South. It is as if the pregnant Negress of the opening of the fifth section of "Kabnis" is the South waiting to birth the book itself as Lewis and ultimately Kabnis (and thus by implication Toomer) recognize their ties to the region. A "womb-song" pulses in the night, as the natural setting of "Cane- and cotton-fields, pine forests, cypress swamps, sawmills, and factories are fecund at her touch" (105). Carrie, too, is a mother figure, caring for the old man, "lovely in her fresh energy of the morning, in the calm untested confidence and nascent maternity which rise from the purpose of her present mission" of providing him with food (115). Carrie recognizes the significance of the old man and his words, for she says, "I've heard that th souls of old folks have a way of seein things" (116). According to Halsey, his sister Carrie has heard the old man say several words, but "mostly one—an like as not cause it was 'sin,'" Halsey explains (106). Throughout this section Kabnis suggests his own desire to use language to speak truth, to write, and he now wonders why the old man, "who died way back there in th 'sixties," is "throwin it in my throat for" (114). Kabnis asks the old man, "An do y think you'll ever see th light of day again, even if you wasnt blind? Do y think youre out of slavery? Huh?" (115). Kabnis cannot accept his kinship with this man. He continues to see himself as separate from the past represented by the cellar and by Father John.

Finally, though, it is as if the old man speaks through Kabnis when Kabnis recognizes his own relationship to the cellar and to the old man's life. At first, when Kabnis defines sin, he describes it in the terms of the old man's world: "It was only a preacher's sin they knew in those old days, an that wasnt sin at all." But Kabnis finally sees the larger implications of the word: "Mind me, th only sin is whats done against th soul." He recognizes, too, the relationship between his race and the sin of slavery: "Th whole world is a conspiracy t sin, especially in America, an against me. I'm th victim of their sin. I'm what sin is" (116). Even in the last few pages of the book, Kabnis struggles against the implications of his realizations, especially when he says to the old man, "So thats your sin. All these years t tell us that th white folks made th Bible lie. Well, I'll be damned. Lewis ought t have been here. You old black fakir—." But Carrie, taking Kabnis's hot cheeks in her cool hands, draws out the fever within him. And with the passing of the fever, Kabnis "crumples. He sinks to his knees before her, ashamed, exhausted" (117).

Although Kabnis's collapse and the living death of the old man may at first seem to suggest the failure of Kabnis's search and thus of Toomer's own self-discoveries, the conclusion of *Cane* suggests promise rather than failure. Out of death comes life. Out of the darkness of the cellar comes a return to life for Kabnis. In the cellar, according to Scruggs and VanDemarr, Kabnis comes face to face with African

American history: "Being down there with Father John, he relives history, and, against his will, he becomes a witness to the continuity of racial oppression." Although a reader would expect Lewis, rather than Kabnis, to be the one who is able to get the old man to speak, Kabnis succeeds because, as Scruggs and Van Demarr have noted, "the real detective cannot be detached and cannot treat the problem to be solved as only a rational puzzle; he will have to be someone like Christ who lives with the lepers and who is himself crippled" (196).

Cane may be a swan-song as Toomer has called it, but the book also was the birthing song of Toomer's creative expression. The end of the book suggests a new beginning: as "light streaks through the iron-barred cellar window," it illuminates and encircles Carrie and Father John. The sun rises outside "from its cradle in the tree-tops of the forest": "Shadows of pines are dreams the sun shakes from its eyes. The sun arises. Gold-glowing child, it steps into the sky and sends a birth-song slanting down gray dust streets and sleepy windows of the southern town" (117). And from that song was born *Cane*—a product of an individual's love-hate relationship with the South, a product of the intense longing for self-knowledge, and the acknowledgement of the necessity of racial and regional pasts.

With its initial publication in 1923, Jean Toomer's *Cane* helped to lay the groundwork for the New Negro Renaissance as it garnered interest and enthusiasm from a generation of writers who were recognizing the potential of their own perspectives on American life and culture. *Cane* took up questions of identity that would be at the focal point of the New Negro Renaissance, questions that revolved around African Americans' relationship to the South. According to Arna Bontemps, "no earlier volume of poetry or fiction or both had come close to expressing the ethos of the negro in the Southern setting as *Cane* did" (187). The book tremendously affected writers such as Langston Hughes, Countee Cullen, and Zora Neale Hurston who were at the focal point of the movement and who were just beginning their careers when *Cane* was first published. Cullen, for example, described the book as "a real race contribution, a classic portrayal of things as they are" (Wintz 75). The book also has been credited with influencing later generations of African American writers, including Ralph Ellison and

Alice Walker. *Cane*'s influence on African American writers would see a resurgence when African American writers rediscovered it during the 1960s. Walker, for one, has been quoted as saying, "I did not read *Cane* until 1967, but it has been reverberating in me to an astonishing degree. *I love it passionately*; could not possibly exist without it" ("Interview" 259).

When Waldo Frank wrote his foreword to the first edition of *Cane* (1923), he claimed for the book a distinguished place in southern literary history. Frank hails the book as "a harbinger of the South's literary maturity." Describing the book as a "chaos of verse, tale, drama," with a "rhythmic rolling shift from lyricism to narrative, from mystery to intimate pathos," Frank suggests that *Cane*'s readers will see a vital, complicated form taking shape out of that chaos. That forming shape, he explains, is much like the ever-evolving South. Frank describes *Cane* as "an aesthetic equivalent of the land" of the South, a region he characterizes as just emerging from "the obsession put upon its minds by the unending racial crisis." In the past, writers had not faced the essential question of race and the South, and had avoided the subject by writing literature characterized as sentimental, exotic, or melodramatic. *Cane*, Frank says, "marks the dawn of direct and unafraid creation" (139–40). In effect, because it deals so forcefully and explicitly with issues of race, the book has had an enduring impact and an enduring place in the Southern Literary Renaissance.

Clearly, *Cane* played a significant role in ushering in the Southern Renaissance. Toomer was one of the first southern writers intensely concerned with the issues generally associated with the renaissance of southern writing, that is, a reexamination of southern identity, the southerner's relationship to the soil, the history and effects of slavery, and the artist's role within the southern community. Although during the renaissance Toomer was not considered part of the modern southern literary movement because it was "whites-only," his contributions have been more fully recognized since. Toomer's achievement is equally important because in its pages, *Cane* not only ties together the essential themes of the southern and New Negro renaissances but also the black and white races into an "eternal purple," a symbol of the profound importance of the South joining once again with the rest of the nation. Toomer faced the essential questions of race and the South, and in doing so, he secured an important place for himself and for *Cane* in the history of southern literature.

Ultimately, though, Toomer saw writing *Cane* as a means to reinvigorate and reform American culture and literature. African Americans could breathe new life into American society, Toomer firmly believed. Nevertheless, he also saw the rural life of the southern black as quickly fading. As he explained in an undated letter to Waldo Frank, probably written in late 1922 or early 1923: "Dont let us fool ourselves, brother: the Negro of the folk-song has all but passed away: the Negro of the emotional church is fading. A hundred years from now these Negroes, if they exist at all will live in art. And I believe that a vague sense of this fact is the driving force behind the art movements directed towards them today. (Likewise the Indian.) America needs these elements. They are passing. Let us grab and hold them while there is still time" (151).

If, as Toomer says, the design of *Cane* is a circle with the curve ending in the poem "Harvest Song," then Toomer himself calls to other African Americans as the circle closes. In "Harvest Song," the persona is tired, weak and cold from reaping the grains of the earth. He has no energy to bind the grain; he hungers, and his throat is dry. The persona strains to hear the voices of other harvesters, voices that might join him to speak not only of the blacks of the rural South but also of their place within America. Toomer calls others in to join his voice, to speak of the vital role of rural southern folk, the vital role of the common man and woman of America.

4 Jesse Stuart

"A FARMER SINGING AT THE PLOW"

Under the two little poplars where Mom used to have her wash-kettle
where I was letting my mule cool and rest from the bitter dust and
hot sun, I wrote:

SIR:
I am a farmer singing at the plow
And as I take my time to plow along
A steep Kentucky hill, I sing my song.

When Jesse Stuart stopped his plow to write this sonnet, which
would be the first in his *Man with a Bull-Tongue Plow,* the moment
was a defining one (*Beyond* 277). He had determined that he would
write poetry as he chose to write poetry—rather than listening to
the advice of a publisher or even a teacher. Believing himself a failure at writing, he decided, "I'm going to be myself and write to suit
myself and the way I damn well please" (*Beyond* 276–77). Like the enduring figure of the southern mountaineer, Stuart was asserting his
independence, his willingness to go it alone. Stuart also expresses
the primary relationship he sees between his work as a writer and his
work as a farmer. His poetry flows from him like the words of a song
to the farmer. The words of his poetry come from the land, from the
ground that he knows in Kentucky. He cultivates his poems like he
cultivates the soil.

This moment was a defining one not only for Stuart the poet but also for Appalachian literature in general. The literature of the Appalachian South was—and remains—distinct from the rest of southern literature. In the nineteenth century, Appalachian literature was typically written by outsiders. Some, such as Anne Newport Royall, wrote of their travels through the region on their way to other parts of the country. Others like Mary Murfree and George Washington Harris lived in Appalachian cities and remained outsiders who wrote of isolated mountain communities and their cultures. Murfree and Harris are perhaps the most prominent figures of nineteenth-century Appalachia, but both looked at the Appalachian world from the outside, with the same eyes as their readers. It was not until several decades into the twentieth century that writers from the southern Appalachian region gained prominence in the publishing world by crafting mountaineer voices that spoke for themselves. The literary voices of Jesse Stuart, James Still, Harriette Arnow, and Thomas Wolfe have long defined the renaissance in the literature of Appalachia. The literature of the region has continued to flourish, with writers like Lee Smith and Mary Lee Settle coming to the forefront. But Stuart's collection of poetry entitled *Man with a Bull-Tongue Plow* remains the distinct beginning of a renaissance in Appalachian literature.

Jesse Stuart's publishing history and awards attest to the significance of his work in the larger realm of American letters. Among the most prolific and most popular American writers of his time, Stuart authored over sixty published volumes. He published at least three hundred short stories, although the actual number is probably closer to five hundred. He received a Guggenheim award, and his work was nominated for a Pulitzer. Kentucky's poet laureate for more than thirty years, he was recognized by the Academy of American Poets in 1955 for his distinguished service to American poetry. Perhaps even better known as a fiction writer than as a poet, Stuart's novel *Taps for Private Tussie* (1943) sold more than two million copies within two years. A Book-of-the-Month selection, *Taps* focused on the effects of World War II on a Kentucky family. A farmer and an educator, as well as a writer, Stuart is probably best known for his *The Thread That Runs So True* (1949), which is based on his years teaching in mountain communities and the struggles he encountered in attempting to educate the children of mountain folk. Despite the fact that only a small body of literary criticism has been written about Stuart's poetry and fiction, his work as a writer made a significant impact in the literary and publishing worlds from the 1940s until well into the 1970s.

The Vanderbilt Agrarians played an important role in the evolution of Stuart's creative voice. After completing his undergraduate degree in 1929 at Lincoln Memorial University in Harrogate, Tennessee, Stuart returned home to Greenup, Kentucky, for a few years to teach school and to write. Originally hoping to attend an Ivy League school for graduate work, Stuart ultimately decided that he wished to study with Robert Penn Warren, John Crowe Ransom, and Donald Davidson. But he never finished a master's degree from Vanderbilt because of his poor grades and his inability (or perhaps unwillingness) to write papers appropriate to the assignments. In his autobiographical *Beyond Dark Hills* (1938), Stuart writes of never having the money to eat three meals a day and of suffering the embarrassment of hearing his own stomach churning from hunger while he listened to Robert Penn Warren lecture on the works of Elizabeth Madox Roberts. A fire in his dormitory destroyed all his possessions, including his master's thesis, bundles of poems, a term paper, and portions of a novel; the blaze also destroyed a good portion of the hopes Stuart seemed to have for achieving the degree.

Stuart left Vanderbilt with a 322-page term paper that would eventually be published as his first prose work. Each year Professor Edwin Mims of the Vanderbilt English Department required students to write an autobiographical piece that most students did not take very seriously because they believed that little had thus far transpired in their lives. Jesse Stuart spent eleven days writing his paper—sometimes through the night. He took portions to Robert Penn Warren, who encouraged him "to keep it up" even if he had "to throw everything else aside" (260). The paper traced Stuart's life in the mountains, telling first of his ancestors, the "tall men" who settled in eastern Kentucky, then moving on to his growing interest in literature and his time at Vanderbilt. According to Stuart, when he submitted the paper to Mims, Mims expressed his aggravation that Stuart had written so many pages for him to read. Mims always read his students' papers from front to back—a task Stuart claimed some professors just would not do. A week passed. On his way to show Warren a poem he had written, Stuart passed by Mims's office. Ushering him in, after an exchange of hard looks, Mims said, "I have been teaching school for forty years and I have never read anything so crudely written and yet beautiful, tremendous, and powerful as that term paper you have written" (262). Mims did not give Stuart a grade for the term paper—part of the reason Stuart did not receive his degree—but with the addition of a final chapter, Stuart published it as *Beyond Dark Hills* in 1938.

Despite Stuart's later claim that he was "in a different university," he found the friendship and encouragement of Vanderbilt professor Donald Davidson to be exceedingly helpful in the establishment of his career. But then Davidson did encourage Stuart to avoid "arty" poems and to write instead of the hill country and its people. Davidson was a thoughtful reader and critic of Stuart's poetry, and he was able to make literary connections for Stuart that were invaluable to his success as a writer. When Davidson wrote Louis Untermeyer about Stuart's work, he spoke glowingly of Stuart's poetry and portrayed Stuart as a mountain poet worthy of validation by the best of American letters. Referring to Stuart as his "mountain friend," Davidson called him "an American Robert Burns. . . the first real poet (aside from ballad makers) ever to come out of the southern mountains" (Foster 55–56).

Like *Beyond Dark Hills*, *Man with a Bull-Tongue Plow* is an autobiography—only in poetry. A collection of 703 sonnets, the work focuses on Stuart's community rather than on the details of his life, telling of the lives of people he knew in his mountain home and people who came before him whose stories he heard told. The book is a tribute to his mountains and its people, describing both the beauty of the place and people and the harshness of their lives in the natural world. Mixing beauty and tragedy, the poems encompass a world that Stuart believed had been left unsung. The place and the people he held dearly in his heart, although as a youth his greatest desire seemed to be to leave the mountains. The poems show the difficult labors of work on the Stuart farm but also reflect the great pride Stuart took in accomplishing a task and his joy at working close to the soil. He writes of his time at Vanderbilt—poor grades and all—and of finally returning home, to visit the cemetery and to tell the stories of those who lay there. In a series of poems included in the collection, Stuart speaks directly to Don Davidson with words about not only the inevitability of death but also the importance of the link between the poetic voice and the earth, a further affirmation of Davidson's agrarian values.

The collection has often been criticized for being too bulky—too many poems on the same subject and too poorly edited. All in all, however, the poetry collection is a book about coming of age, of struggling with the inevitability of death and recognizing the importance of an attachment to and acceptance of place and family. At times, Stuart dips into portraits of the ideal, as in "The Trail." Also included in *Beyond Dark Hills,* the poem was written as Stuart sat on a stump on a December evening after his return home from Lincoln Memorial. The trail of the poem's title leads him to his "mountain hut" where he knows his supper is waiting and where he and his parents and siblings—"seven strong"—will "soon be gathered . . . To eat and drink, forget the field and plow." The persona of the poem explains that after the family has finished supper, they will "sing and play, / And dance and tell the tales of warriors old." He remembers the words of his grandsires who said, "Live happy now for soon you're sleeping cold." And they do.

> We do live happy, don't you ever doubt,
> We drink our wild-grape wine and apple gin,
> We hear the storm winds blow the leaves about,
> We wonder if the cattle are housed in.

Stuart prays that the "Dear path of earth" or the trail he follows will "lead me the olden way . . . And let me keep a heart of sumac clay; / And in its core an image of my hut." Saying he is no better than his ancestors before him who now lie buried in the Kentucky earth, he knows that "Within these hills there are no prison bars / To cage the wiry flesh and mind of me . . . I am the blood of those now seeking rest, / Pioneers now gone to meet and conquer dawn." He is the vital life of those who have come before him, his ancestors who settled this land, made their homes. He wishes to always keep at his core a spirit like that of his ancestors, one tied to the earth, "sumac clay" to the very heart of him (*Beyond* 247–48).

Man with a Bull-Tongue Plow revolves around Stuart's own personal struggle between his desire to flee the Kentucky hills and the powerful feelings that draw him back home. Claiming to want to keep his struggle a private one, he writes that he did not want people to know both the passion and the hatred he had for his home. The same story is often heard from educated individuals from rural areas, southern or not. Stuart writes that he wanted to see what lay beyond the hills; he wanted "to taste of life," one he "tasted of . . . from books and steel and the merry-go-round." But when he went beyond those hills and left his home far behind, he realized "It was not sweet like the life in the hills" (*Beyond* 183). The book, with its flaws, is the work of a young writer, overly concerned with the prospect of inevitable death, expressing his romantic feelings for several different women, fleeing his home community then returning with a satisfaction that this is the place he belongs. *Man with a Bull-Tongue Plow* brought Stuart success. The book jump-started his career and quickly led to a Guggenheim fellowship that allowed him to study in Scotland.

Beyond Dark Hills and *Man with a Bull-Tongue Plow* together show the evolution of Stuart's poetic voice, a voice defined by his relationship to the soil. In *Beyond*, Stuart writes that there is poetry within "the great prolific earth in Kentucky hills" that he plows. Poetry, he says, is "the very blood of me!" "So close akin" to him, poetry haunts him. It is poetry that he "see[s] and smell[s] and feel[s] in the spring blossoms and the budding of the leaves and in the changing seasons of the year. Poetry that speaks its messages . . . in the flower-scented winds of spring among the wild crab-apple blossoms and the snow-white percoon; poetry I hear in the winds of autumn sighing among the dry clusters of turning leaves for the summer that will not come again; poetry I hear in the moaning winds of winter in the leafless boughs that moan for the old life lying beneath the snow creating a womb wherein violets will peep with the first bird calls for spring!" (315).

In the opening sonnet in *Man with a Bull-Tongue Plow*, Stuart speaks of his poems as songs sung at the plow. He equates his poems with the physical aspects of nature, with aspects of the natural world—not of the world beyond the dark hills. They are "basket songs" "woven from the words / Of corn and crickets, trees and men and birds." He sings his "lays like singing corn, / And flute[s] them like a fluting gray corn-bird" that he can pipe "like a hunter's horn—." These are songs he has heard his entire life. But, with perhaps a mixture of embarrassment and a recognition that he is speaking with an independent voice for a place and people he knows and loves, he writes, "these crude strains no critic can call art." These are not songs the "Sir" to whom he addresses the poem would care to hear. In Sonnet 3, he explains that he writes of the "color of the clay" and the men who will work the fields: "I speak of men that live in my lifetime, / And I speak of the men of yesterday. / I do not care to know if this is art— / These common words born in a common heart."

Stuart describes the poet as the plowman who digs into the earth, lives by the seasons of the earth, harvests a crop from the land, and receives his inspiration from the soil. Stuart himself is often taking up the pen (or whatever materials he can find) to write his poetry as he plows the fields of his family's Kentucky farm. He intimately intertwines the craft of writing poetry with plowing the earth's fields when he says, for example, "I plowed the soil. I planted the grain. I read books. I wrote poetry" (*Beyond* 221) or "I shall return to plow and spin my rhymes" (Sonnet 439). He speaks to Don Davidson specifically in Sonnet 677, saying, "I did not ask [the poems] come. / But I sat by the plow and wrote them down." Stuart describes the summer of the year and of a man's life as "The time to make his bread and sing his song, / For winter brings white-sheeted hills and gloom" (Sonnet 672). He describes other poets as taking up the task of plowing: "Other poets will plow and cut the brush / And earn their bread by the sweat from their brow / Behind two steady mules and turning-plow!" (Sonnet 19). And he reminds Davidson that in death he will "not get to use a bull-tongue plow" (Sonnet 687). As "Proud poet of the rustic life" (Sonnet 657), he is full of words because he has lived that rustic life and is "unafraid to gut and bone" (Sonnet 659). "I carried brains and baskets filled with words," Stuart says, "I spun my rhymes—(To me it was no task)— / Words were to me I've said as skies to birds" (Sonnet 677).

Poetry writing is not something that one must be educated into, Stuart discovered after failing to receive his master's degree at Vanderbilt. The poems just come to him as he plows the fields, as the inspiration flows from the earth, he says in Sonnet 689 in which he addresses Davidson: "I learned it did not take a Ph.D. / To walk between the handles of a plow," or, as he says in Sonnet 690, "to interpret wind in the pine tree." Poetry is not something he waits to happen but something that engulfs him. In *Beyond Dark Hills,* he explains that "It was just in me to write poetry and I did not suppress the desire. Poetry took me along. It made me its servant. I couldn't handle poetry . . . Poetry puts you down and makes you write . . . You have to be your own self." Poetry will come first in your life—even before the term papers that you will let "go to hell," and it will make you "lie to your teachers" (232–33).

But Stuart also suggests the aggravation he felt at the response he received to his education beyond his Kentucky hills. With this aggravation also seems to have come his determination to define his poetic voice within the context of his mountain home. He rejects, too, a poetic life shaped by someone else's decisions, views, and values. "Better to sing of life from where I start—," he writes in Sonnet 20, "From mountain folks and from Kentucky hills. / Better to sing and never ask a dime / For ruggedness I spin into a rhyme, / For I can live—to hell with all your gold." He has chosen to write what he wants to write—and to ignore the responses from the outside world. He knows he can find a living in the hills, be independent, and write as he chooses: "I know I'm strong enough to work the soil. / My friends, this bard will not be bought and sold / Since he can make his bread by honest toil!"

Implicit in the development of Stuart's literary voice is his choice of persona: the independent, rugged, earth-plowing man of the hills. This persona frees Stuart from an academic world and a literary marketplace that question the validity of his subjects. It grants him the ability to write what he chooses for an audience whom he chooses, but Stuart's hillman persona is firmly grounded in the tradition of

Jefferson's yeoman. No longer is the Appalachian figure the Other of Murfree's or Harris's stories—isolated people who lead lives distinct from those of readers. Instead, Stuart crafts his hillmen so that they represent humanity at large—facing the fact of passing generations, looking to the natural world for strength and beauty, clinging to home and family. Stuart's hillmen are distinctly American figures, although they have long remained unacknowledged by America. Their ancestors were hardy pioneers who traveled across the mountains to settle, people who ultimately became bound to the eastern Kentucky soil as they cleared the land and plowed their fields. Stuart is part of the achievement of their blood.

Stuart is thus tied to this land not only because he was born and raised there but also because his ancestors have farmed its soil, because he intimately knows the people of his mountain community, and because he ultimately makes a decision to return home to those hills. He says in Sonnet 305, "It is my land and I am part of it— / I think I'm clay from in the heart of it— / My land." Stuart's poetic persona is forever connected to the land of Kentucky. The flesh of his body is "eternal Kentuckian": "Walking among her hills, breathing her air; / Plowing her soil, feeling her wind and sun . . . Surely, I am eternal Kentuckian—." His Kentucky ancestors were "sons and daughters of the soil." "My people," he writes, "have lived here all of their days, / Plowed the same soil, felt the same wind and sun . . . And made their living by an honest toil." There is meaning in knowing that his "flesh will not go down eternal dust," but is specifically "Kentuckian's dust" (Sonnet 320). He sees himself as forever tied to this land and this land to him because "This land is mine, for I am part of it. / I am the land, for it is part of me" (Sonnet 7). He writes of being kin to the earth: "I am a brother to the hillside trees. I am a brother to the mountain loam" (Sonnet 410).

Stuart recognizes, too, the primacy of the land, for it provides food and from it comes the "strength of life" and the "beauty of the flowers." According to Sonnet 128, "The land is all—the golden locust soil." Stuart speaks of his relationship to the land not in terms of property deeds but instead as one who is connected to the soil through his kinship with the earth because of his humanity. The trees—the gum, the oak, and the pine—all "belong" to him. He owns this land not in a legal sense, but in the sense that he is spiritually a part of the earth. The workings of Nature also reflect the roots of humanity, for the "passionate surging of the elements" suggests the "passions of primitive men!" There is a draw to the earth for Stuart—a "deep-blood call"—from which he says he cannot run away (Sonnet 168). And when he is far from his mountain home, according to Sonnet 9, he hears the call of the mountain winds and feels drawn homeward. The "call to earth" may pound on his brain, but digging in that dirt allows him freedom from "man and work and work." In dirt there is comfort and solace, and "rest comes better after one must work." Stuart points out that human beings are often called by the sound of money, but "The call to earth one seldom hears at all." When the earth does call, it calls from deep within one's being: "when sap stirs in trees blood in my veins / Runs swift as flooded water in Spring streams" (Sonnet 167). The earth has healing powers, for "verse from the soil," he explains in Sonnet 209, is "a good balm for ills." Throughout the sonnet collection, Stuart points to the inevitability of death and the ultimate return of the human being to the soil. He writes of Earth's prison that drinks the blood of human beings it has created and whom Stuart wishes might live immortally. He speaks of the decay of human flesh after burial in graphic terms, but ultimately Stuart recognizes the human's return to the earth as inevitable and as part of a larger plan within Nature.

Within the order of Nature, Stuart found an order for his creative works. He writes in *Beyond Dark Hills* of being told by an instructor that in writing a short story, he should "follow a skeleton." But when he considers this suggestion, he says, "I always thought of a man's white bones dangling in the wind without flesh on the body, without blood in the veins, without life, color, love, dreams." The idea of the skeleton only conjures up an image of a dead oak tree with its branches broken, its bark sloughing off, and its boughs bare of leaves. *Beyond Dark Hills* describes Stuart's growth as a writer, including his assessment that he should use his own voice, make his own judgments about his creative work, and let the words flow as they will. In order to attain such strength, he taps into his mountaineer heritage of independence and self-sustenance. "I just didn't like skeletons and never could use them," he concludes. "I did the story the way I wanted to. Why not . . . who was writing the story? Wasn't it my thought?" His stories, he believed, should be "a slice of life lived by my own hill people. They didn't live and die by a skeleton with crow deposits for a climax either . . . I would write as they lived to be honest about it. That was my skeleton and the blossoms for the branches were words I thought would fit" (310–11).

The poet-farmer who plows the fields with a bull-tongue plow has a unique relationship with the earth and thus creates a literature of particularly high value, according to Stuart. Although people from outside Stuart's mountain community may see the mountaineers as "children of the night" because many of them are illiterate, the earth is their book: "Their education is a book of soil— / They are men taught to work and pray and fight." "Let them be children of the darker night," Stuart writes (Sonnet 394). The land itself is a scroll that the winds can read. People are bound together in their communities because they face the elements of nature together as farmers. In effect, they become isolated from each other only when they leave nature. This close relationship with the soil, according to Stuart, ultimately has the greatest of benefits. Even in the midst of a desolate winter that envelops the land for months and months, there is a security. As he thinks of the bitter winds that blew outside his family home, he remembers, too, that his family felt secure because they had preserved the "fruits of the land" and stocked them in the house. Rather than remaining in their home in isolation, they helped neighbors who needed their aid. But they were prepared because they lived close to the soil: "And cozily we sat by our fireside / And ate of corn and supped of berry-wine; / We sat and let the snow-world drift outside; / We sat and watched through frosted window panes / The snow flakes drifting through green tops of pine" (Sonnet 8).

Life close to the soil is one of both dependence and independence. The farmer sows and reaps his own grain according to the seasons of Nature. Beyond the dark hills, there are "parasites sucking the blood from his veins to live." Stuart agrees that life in the hills may be a difficult one, but the tradeoff is worth it. It is still one's "own lot." As a result of these difficulties, "Life in the hills would make one sturdy and independent. The handles of the plow make one free" (*Beyond* 183). Tilling the sod also brings one close to Nature, or as Stuart suggests, close to God. Taking up the plow can also bring one peace, Stuart explains in a sonnet written to Donald Davidson. Peace will come because the farmer at the plow is close to God. Stuart found that beyond the hills, people did not worship God as they do in the mountains of eastern Kentucky. When he went beyond the hills, he was told, "there was nothing in this game of God." Desperately wanting to be a part of that world, he tried to believe there was no God, but when he returned to the hills, he saw once again from the viewpoint of the mountain people. "I found," he says, "the great consolation of God in the beauty of the hills. Call God a God of love or a God of beauty. Say that God is in the wind, that God is in the dead leaves flying over the September hills in Kentucky, but don't leave God out." Stuart came to see God as "an ancient song among the minds of many people." He came to realize, too, that in the hills, the people still relied on God, the "great force that drew them together." God was the one who "called the inner something of their bodies, greater than flesh and bone, to walk out under the trees and pray" (183–84).

Stuart often refers to those who are educated and intellectual as living in the air, but he maintains throughout *Beyond Dark Hills* and *Man with a Bull-Tongue Plow* that it is through living close to the soil, not in the clouds, that one can reach the highest spiritual level. When he went beyond the hills to receive an education, he lived in the air, but once he returned home to the earth, it soon became clear that that sort of education was superficial, "damn tommyrot." "Come back home and put your feet on the earth again. See how you feel." An education can't lead you to God—it can't tell you anything about God. "Get close to the soil and know Him. Get educated and forget life. That's what you'll do if you're not careful" (242). In Sonnet 147, he says to the soil of the earth that he believes there will never be a time when he will achieve such notoriety that he will be "wreathed in little oak-leaf fame." He will not fly in song to the heights of the mountains because he had grown "too close the earth in sterile soil." He decides that he will remain grounded, and if by chance he "should drift singing to the skies," he won't forget Kentucky, the land he loves, "a paradise," "where starlight and shadow fill the eyes."

Farming the hills also offers the most poetic of subjects for a writer like Stuart. Stuart writes of one hillman, Bill Ludlow, and his desire for his son to work in an office, to make a living "with a pencil behind [his] ear." Bill doesn't recognize the value of the life he and his son lead in the mountains. Stuart addresses Ludlow as he addresses the reader, reminding him that he should envy the snake that rides upon the ground because "it rubs the soil closer than you." Life lived close to the soil may seem bitter, but in that life is also "the greatest sweetness in the world." Pointing, in particular, to the life and work of Robert Frost, Stuart tells the illiterate Ludlow that he should "know" Frost: "He is a farmer. But he tells you something about the soil in poetry" (*Beyond* 210-11).

"There is a beauty in the soil that is unsurpassed. There is tragedy, too, in the dark hills, Bill Ludlow," Stuart writes (211). He tells, in particular, of a man who left his pregnant wife at home to take whiskey to the city to sell to pay for a doctor for his wife. The town was thirty miles from home, and the man and his wife did not know when the baby would arrive. Carefully packing the whiskey on his mule, the man rode to town where he sold the whiskey and then brought the doctor home with him on the mule. But they arrived too late. The man's wife had tried to have the baby by herself, and both baby and mother had died in childbirth. Then hungry hounds and hogs had broken into the house and eaten from the corpses of the dead mother and baby. How can one ignore the great power of the stories the land holds, Stuart asks Ludlow. Likewise, in *Beyond Dark Hills* Stuart remembers the story of a Mrs. Waters who committed suicide after the birth of her ninth child. The Waters family had debts and a mortgage on their property and were getting a low price on tobacco. Sick with worry about the debt and the possibility they might lose their home, Mrs. Waters "got nervous" and tried to kill herself, first with a butcher's knife and then with a rope. Her husband took her to a doctor, who said she was insane. Planning to send her to an asylum the following day, they put her in the jail for the night—the only place they believed she might remain safe from doing herself harm. That night she burned herself to death by wrapping herself in blankets and setting the blankets on fire. She left nine children—ranging from seventeen years to about two months—to fend for themselves (218).

Within this place of dark tragedy, Stuart also saw great beauty in the mountains, in the falling leaves, in the works of Nature. "The heavens [may] declare the glory of God," he writes but goes on to say that he didn't fully understand the meaning of that sentence until he left the mountains. Poignantly, Stuart describes this place: "It was the land of tobacco, the land of God, the land of oak trees, the land of beauty, the land of desolation, the home of tragic living and the home of the sweetness of life. Great dark hills, with life among them, with death among them. Great hills, green millions of years ago, that give us food, shelter, and warmth in life and take us back to their bosom in the end" (219).

Stuart saw poetry not only in the hills but also in human beings. He wonders, in *Beyond Dark Hills*, how Nature could create such "wonderful" human beings and then let them die. "Poetry, how can these wonderful human beings pass? . . . Can't we get a few in song? . . . Can't we catch a fleeting glimpse of them as they pass from the fluffy green of spring to the dying autumn grass? Can't we do these things while it is my season and my generation and before the glorious or the tragic end!" He sees himself as Poetry's medium: "You flow through my veins and through the gateway of my brain!" (315). Poetry is the means to preserving his memories and the lives of these people, as he emphasizes in Sonnet 611, where first he says to the Earth that he does not fear death because he knows that death must ultimately come to all. But he has his "little part" to play "among the lowly folks, for I belong / To them." It is for them that he writes, that he sings his song and crafts his "rustic art." Believing this to be the ultimate purpose and aim of his art, Stuart suggests, too, the significant role and thus the necessity of what he does. His art is part of Nature as the song of any bird and the beauty of any flower.

So that he might preserve his world within poetry, a number of poems in *Man with a Bull-Tongue Plow* concern the lives of individuals who lived and died in his hill community. In *Beyond Dark Hills*, Stuart says that he wished to give voices to the dead. "Why not let all these dead speak?" he asks. He goes to the cemetery, a place he knows well, because he saw many of these people carried there in their coffins and buried. "I let them speak. . . . I write and write and write for them . . . The dreams that have come and the dreams that have faded." In effect, he writes their words for them. He tells of the lives of people he actually knew and of those who shared the same community generations before. By telling their stories, their lives then "have passed through the pages of a book." He speaks for all of them—"even the worst of them"—because all people have at least some good in them when they truly speak from their hearts. Stuart puts himself into their places and tries to speak for them with honesty. He seems to want to return a favor to the people of the hills and their place because, as he says, the hills "had always stood by me" (307).

Man with a Bull-Tongue Plow and *Beyond Dark Hills* both show the influence of ballads and old-time mountain music. Quoting mountain songs and crafting poems that recall those songs figure in his effort to preserve the culture and arts of his region. He recognized that while his education from schools beyond the mountains might teach him to look down with disdain upon all things associated with the mountains, including old-time music and mountain ballads, he would always love the mountains and its people, "the happiest people in the world." "I'm not getting along very well with my education," Stuart states emphatically, if the end result is losing his "love and appreciation" for his home (241–42).

When Stuart returns to Vanderbilt in *Beyond Dark Hills*, he leaves a land he both loved and hated, but he wants to preserve in his poetry its people and places. The poems capture his memories of the people he knew, the plowed earth that he farmed, and the trees and plants of the woods, so that he can return home through his own writing. He recognizes the necessity of preserving these memories for himself, and for his community, for the old way of life is fading: "these quiet things . . . are the best after all. There is something good about the old country life that is passing. It is the real sweetness of living down against the soil. And that life will never come again" (160). Both *Man with a Bull-Tongue Plow* and *Beyond Dark Hills* are pastoral works, attempting to capture a fleeting way of life but also representing the countryside as an ideal.

"These quiet things," "the old country life," seem forgotten by America. Although Stuart claims a significant stature for the hillmen as the descendents of "men and women wrought of finest clay" who traveled in oxen cart over the Kentucky Wilderness Road (Sonnet 592), he also emphasizes their role within America at large. It is finally American soil unto which he and his hillmen will return in death: they will become "Dust of America" and lie beneath the skin and ribs of America (Sonnet 600). "America, why don't you speak for us! / America, why don't you speak to us!" he asks.

> Speak out for us—let poets rise and sing,
> But not of butterflies and white-moth wing;
> But let them sing of earth and men of power,
> And let them sing of seasons and the flower—
> To hell with singers' sentimental songs,
> Let them sing for men where they belong.
> Give us a singer that will sing for us—
> The truth of us—
> (Sonnet 553)

Stuart calls here for an acceptance of the Southern Appalachian region and its people. He wants an acknowledgement that, yes, indeed, Southern Appalachia is an American region worthy of song, worthy of praise like other parts of the country. He hopes, too, that his "rustic art" will be appreciated, that some will "keep his futile tunes in brain and heart" after he has died, "When he is quiet and sleeps beneath the clay / And has no thought of his past yesterday." He hopes for a young poet to follow him who "guides his plow along / And plows upon the quiet Kentucky clay" (Sonnet 2).

When *Man with a Bull-Tongue Plow* was first published, the publisher made a concerted effort to show the relationship between the author of the poems and the specifically American earth about which he wrote. The jacket of the book reads, "Jesse Stuart is an extension of the soil on which he lives and works; he seems to be a part of the earth itself . . . This book was born out of the American soil, and it is imperishable." An American perspective for the book might have helped to increase sales of the volume, but the publisher's note claims for a southerner a decidedly American perspective that is borne out in Stuart's own attempts to link his region to an American landscape and to identify his regional history within the context of an American history.

Stuart's hillman is thus an American as well as a southerner. And he is an American born from the abiding principles in American democracy and in the primacy of the common man and his worth as an individual. As Stuart writes in Sonnet 696, he knows that he "may not have been a builder of the nation . . . just one of a hundred millions." He claims for himself a tradition bound within the figure of the common man. But that man has great value, for as Stuart says to Donald Davidson in the poem, he is "Lover of earth and trees and blackberry blossoms, / And a one-horse scrap of land." He is a man of the earth, a man of individualism and independence, a man of worth—the American farmer who lives close to the soil.

5 Marriage and Female Labor

WOMEN'S NOVELS OF THE 1930S SOUTH

When Edna Pontellier commits suicide at the end of Kate Chopin's *The Awakening* (1899), readers are left with more questions than answers about Edna's search for independence and her struggle to achieve some sense of individual identity distinct from her duties as wife and mother. Perhaps at the end of the novel Edna is finally successful in choosing her own future. But how can she be called a success when she takes her own life? Edna may be trapped within a societal framework that forces her onto the southern lady's pedestal, but many present-day readers wonder why Edna could not go on living—leave New Orleans and choose a more humble role as seamstress or as teacher. The tragedy is that she doesn't believe she has the options.

By the 1930s in the South, as the region faced poverty intensified by the Great Depression, southern writers increasingly let the southern lady down from a pedestal and put her to work. With the matter of woman suffrage settled the decade before in the United States, and because of the economics of the times, the myths surrounding southern womanhood were noticeably shifting. Even Margaret Mitchell's Scarlett O'Hara was forced to assume the role of caretaker of Tara and the head of her family's household. Perhaps one reason that *Gone with the Wind* and its movie version were so popular in the 1930s was because readers and viewers who were enduring the years of the Great Depression actually understood Scarlett's struggles for survival. Scarlett's plight was indeed like that faced by many white southern women of the 1930s, not because they no longer enjoyed the glory of a mythologized southern plantation but because they too faced the everyday reality of providing for their families. In this new mythology of the modern South, women went into the fields and there discovered new versions of themselves.

Although the Great Depression affected women in the South as much as the Civil War had by pushing many into working outside the home for their family's survival, the depression also pushed many women out of the work force. Women lost jobs they had struggled to attain because many people believed that in tough economic times, men should have the jobs rather than the women. Nevertheless, the southern woman's role within society definitely underwent a change with the Nineteenth Amendment to the U.S. Constitution, which gave women the right to vote. Increasingly, southern women had opportunities, but they still faced the complexities of a southern society that claimed to protect southern womanhood as an institution only worthy of the pedestal. The ideal of southern womanhood—for both black and white women—remained essentially a life led within a domestic realm and one that allowed a woman few choices. But how could the white mill worker in North Carolina or the white farm laborer in Georgia fit into that mold? Or the black housewife who every day faced the challenges of cooking, washing, gardening, and raising her children?

Woman's work, woman's labor, and the role of marriage in a woman's life were increasingly scrutinized in the 1930s by southern women writers such as Evelyn Scott, Julia Peterkin, Margaret Mitchell, and Zora Neale Hurston, as well as Olive Dargan, who wrote under the name Fielding Burke. Work for women was increasingly tied to questions not only of a woman's right to work outside the home, but also of the value of her work within the home, her right to choose marriage and a career or between marriage and career, and her right to choose life without children by using contraception (even within marriage). According to Laura Hapke in *Daughters of the Great Depression,* for example, Margaret Mitchell depicts Scarlett as a woman making such a decision about the fate of her own body. Scarlett's choice, says Hapke, is life without children, for the death of Scarlett's daughter Bonnie "both unmans Rhett and represents in its way Scarlett's ultimate refusal to mother" (216). The complications of career, marriage, and motherhood were difficult ones during the 1930s—ones that southern women writers were just beginning to address to any great degree.

In the first decades of the twentieth-century, the traditional coming-of-age stories for southern women revolved around finding love and then marrying; in the 1930s these evolved into stories about a woman's search for self outside marriage. Although the framework of love and marriage generally remained, the woman characters in these works are increasingly allowed to make those choices themselves. A typical pattern seems to revolve around the number three—three men, that is. In many ways, Olive Dargan's novel about the Gastonia mill strike entitled *Call Home the Heart* (1932) and other novels such as Zora Neale Hurston's *Their Eyes Were Watching God* (1937)—even Margaret Mitchell's *Gone with the Wind* (1936)—follow similar patterns of organization and meaning. Dargan's Ishma, Hurston's Janie, and Mitchell's Scarlett are each involved with three different men, sometimes in marriage and sometimes not. Through their relationships with these men, the women finally discover growth, individual selfhood, and opportunity for themselves as individuals, and ultimately they make their own choices about their own fates.

What plays a key role in these books is the role of woman's work—inside the home and out. In her mountain home, Dargan's Ishma feels run-down and unfulfilled by farm life with her husband, Britt. Although Ishma leaves Britt for Rad, who represents monetary security—a house with an inside toilet and four rooms—ultimately Britt and Ishma's mountains call her home. After a period of being attracted to the ideals and intellectualism of Dr. Unthank, a major player in the labor uprising, Ishma decides to return to the mountains, and to Britt, and plans to bring the mill children and workers to the mountains in the summers to provide them with relief from their harsh working conditions. Likewise, Hurston frames a story about a woman who first finds monetary security in marriage to Logan Killicks—the only man in the community who has a piano. When he wants to work her like a mule in the fields, she throws aside her apron to marry Jody Starks, the mayor of Eatonville, who will put her on a pedestal. Years later when the older Jody dies, Janie is free from a relationship that separated her from the community: she was the mayor's wife, the keeper of his store who was not allowed to go out onto the porch with the townspeople to hear their tales. When Janie marries Tea Cake, she finds a relationship where she can be an equal. The two enjoy being together, not only the play of their relationship but also their work together in the farm rows in the Everglades. Scarlett, likewise, first loves Ashley because of the Old South ways that he represents, but she marries her sister's beau in order to save Tara, and finally she marries Rhett out of love and passion. The turbulence of this marriage for love—as everyone must know—lasts well beyond the book, for "tomorrow is another day." But a continuous strain in the book is Scarlett's attachment to the land, her relationship to Tara. "'Tis the only thing in this world that lasts," her father reminds her, "and don't you be forgetting it! 'Tis the only thing worth working for, worth fighting for—worth dying for" (38–39). She doesn't forget his advice, not even at the end of the book when she pledges to return home to Tara, where she can "stand it then" that Rhett has left her (1024). Scarlett returns to a place that she has helped to transform to ensure its survival. Tara will survive in the postwar South because Scarlett has remade the plantation into a yeoman farm.

All three women characters thus find renewal by entering the natural world. Although Janie obviously is not fulfilled in her marriage to Logan who would like to have her plowing the fields beside him, her relationship with Tea Cake grows wild and tangled when they go to the Everglades to work as farm laborers. There is obviously no reason for them to take on such work—Janie has enough money in the bank—but Tea Cake suggests they "do somethin' crazy." Although Janie does have to suffer Tea Cake's moment of infidelity as they work down the rows of crops, she finds in the crop rows an equality with a man that she did not experience with Logan or with Jody in the store. Although Ishma feels beaten down by farm labor, by the end of the book she tells Britt, "Life was hard up here [in the mountains], the Lord knows, but when I looked back at it from down yonder, I thought that if I were in one corn row and you in another, I could hoe and hoe and never get tired if the row was as long as forever" (427). The pampered Scarlett finds that her responsibility as caretaker of

Tara places her in a role not traditionally assigned to the belle, and she gains a strength that comes from her relationship to the earth. Rather than representing the land as a feminine entity cared for by the master, Mitchell's Scarlett displaces the male figure who is traditionally the caretaker of the southern land. All three women find sustenance and survival through their attachments to the natural world. The view in all three books, however, is decidedly romantic, idealized, but the women have the ability to see the necessity of making their own choices about their own fates, their work, and their loves. The strength to make those decisions comes from the intimate tie these women have or create with the southern soil. In effect, each is transformed by this bond with the southern earth.

Janie, for example, is a farm laborer who doesn't need to work. She asks, "When do de job open up, Tea Cake," that is, when does their work on the muck begin, noting that "Everybody round here look lak dey waitin' too." Tea Cake explains that they are waiting for the "boss-man" to locate sufficient seed for the bushels they will plant. "Dis ain't no game fuh pennies," according to Tea Cake, because "Po' man ain't got no business at de show" (124). Those who come looking for work picking the crops are in search of work to put food on their tables. The migrant workers are generally people who are experiencing great need and suffering: "All night, all day, hurrying in to pick beans. Skillets, beds, patched up spare inner tubes all hanging and dangling from the ancient cars on the outside and hopeful humanity, herded and hovered on the inside, chugging on to the muck. People ugly from ignorance and broken from being poor" (125). In contrast, Janie and Tea Cake spend their time during the off-season making "little trips to Palm Beach, Fort Myers and Fort Lauderdale for their fun" (139). Janie doesn't work in the fields until Tea Cake tells her he misses her when he is working and she is at home. Still, he prefers her not to work so she can "get her rest" and be able to enjoy evening activities with him, such as the fire dances (146).

Janie's full immersion into this world does not come, however, until she joins the workers in the fields. The landscape of the Everglades is described as larger than life, abundant with vegetation that entangles and an earth so rich that the life it sustains seems to grow out of control with no set boundaries. It is a place of potential but also represents the dramatic change in Janie's life—with all the confusion that comes with new possibilities. "To Janie's strange eyes everything in the Everglades was big and new," Hurston tells us, just like the new life that Tea Cake brings to her in their relationship of romance, adventure, and equality: "Big Lake Okechobee, big beans, big cane, big weeds, big everything. Weeds that did well to grow waist high up the state were eight and often ten feet tall down there. Ground so rich that everything went wild. Volunteer cane just taking the place. Dirt roads so rich and black that a half mile of it would have fertilized a Kansas wheat field. Wild cane on either side of the road hiding the rest of the world. People wild too" (123). This new earth not only provides a sustenance for which Janie longs, but it also invigorates and renews her.

This place is also where Janie comes closest to God. Although not a religious book, *Their Eyes Were Watching God* does hint at the intimate bond between nature and spirit. It is in the tribulations and trials of the hurricane that the people look upward, "their eyes straining against crude walls and their souls asking if He meant to measure their puny might against His." God is connected in the book to light, to truth when Janie says that "It's so many people never seen de light at all. Ah wuz fumblin' round and God opened de door" (151). God "opened the door" for her in the Everglades, where she is for a time part of a community that sets her on equal terms with everyone else—especially in regard to economics and gender. She figuratively reaps the bounty of the "crops" she has planted in this new relationship with Tea Cake.

In a similar fashion, Mitchell represents Scarlett O'Hara's postwar Tara as an idyllic landscape linked to a yeoman tradition—not to the planter tradition represented by the grave of Gerald O'Hara. Scarlett's Tara is a place of peace and abundance of a different sort: "Tara, at sunrise, looked loved, well tended and at peace, for all that its master lay dead . . . The garden with its rows of corn, bright-yellow squash, butter beans and turnips was well weeded and neatly fenced with split-oak rails. The orchard was cleared of underbrush and only daisies grew beneath the long rows of trees. The sun picked out with faint glistening the apples and the furred pink peaches half hidden in the green leaves. Beyond lay the curving rows of cotton, still and green under the gold of the new sky. The ducks and chickens were waddling and strutting off toward the fields, for under the bushes in the soft plowed earth were found the choicest worms and slugs. Scarlett's heart swelled with affection and gratitude to Will who had done all of this" (695).

With the help of Will Benteen, a poor white who fought in the Civil War and who ultimately marries Scarlett's sister Suellen, Tara is transformed from southern plantation to yeoman farm. As Mitchell tells us, "Tara's bloom was not the work of a planter-aristocrat, but of the plodding, tireless 'small farmer' who loved his land." Now Tara was a "'two horse' farm"—"not the lordly plantation of other days with pastures . . . stretching as far as eye could see." Quite symbolically, as Scarlett views the morning beauty of this "two horse farm," her father's body is being prepared for burial. After drinking heavily, Tara's "lord" died attempting to jump his horse over a fence. Despite her sorrow, Scarlett believes now that she can look to the future with a certainty that it might hold some promise. What she concludes as she looks over the landscape that is "good" is that the years of the ground lying fallow have actually allowed the soil to become richer (695–96).

Scarlett recognizes, too, that without this transformation of Tara from lordly plantation to two-horse farm, Tara would have been lost. Numerous other plantations in Georgia have returned to the wild because planters were unable to hold back the growth of seedling pines and blackberry brambles. Will had been able to keep these two "enemies of Georgia planters" at bay, so they "had not stealthily taken garden and pasture and cotton field and lawn and reared themselves insolently by the porches of Tara" (695–96). Scarlett and Will are able to save Tara from Nature and from the Yankees and carpetbaggers because they both recognized that the plantation South was no more.

Elizabeth Jane Harrison describes Scarlett's relationship with Will Benteen as an "alliance . . . made possible by their difference in social status," arguing that if Scarlett remains at Tara to farm with Will, then she will not be able to lay claim to the title of southern lady. The southern belle, Harrison explains, must not marry below her social level because with such a marriage comes loss of economic and social status. According to Harrison, such a marriage topples the belle off her pedestal. Scarlett "resists identifying" with southern belles who marry Yankees or poor whites. In effect, Mitchell marries Scarlett's "stand-in," her sister Suellen, to Will Benteen and thus "solves this postwar class dilemma" (57–58).

Despite Scarlett's disinterest in Will as a possible husband for herself, however, Scarlett recognizes the significance of what they have built together: "Between herself and Will, they had done a good job. They had held off the Yankees, the Carpetbaggers and the encroachments of Nature." Scarlett values the yeoman ideals that Will represents. Although she believes Will would have a difficult time without her help at Tara, Scarlett "admired and respected his independence." As future brother-in-law and "man of the house," Will plans "to stand on his own efforts." For all that he has done for Tara, Scarlett believes Will is "something the Lord had provided" (696).

When Scarlett and Grandma Fontaine speak about Scarlett's willingness to allow Suellen to marry Will, Grandma reacts by saying, "Others would say you [Scarlett] were letting down bars that ought never be lowered one inch" (707). Scarlett does not believe that Will is "quality." By Robillard standards, her sister is, indeed, "coming down in the world." But Scarlett recognizes Will's honesty, his loyalty, his patience and his hard work (707–78). In fact, Scarlett approves of the marriage and cannot understand why her grandmother expects her to automatically interpret the situation in the same way that she does. Scarlett seems to be developing the same kind of independence she recognizes in Will—one not compatible with the image of the belle. Likewise, she seems to have come about this independent spirit in part through her work with Will and in part because of her recognition that she must face reality. Her world has changed and so has her reaction to it.

The evolution of a woman's selfhood in *Gone with the Wind* therefore seems to correspond directly to a woman's connection to the southern earth and whether or not that soil is a fertile one. Likewise, childbearing is also significantly present or absent in women's writings of the 1930s because of this relationship. In *Call Home the Heart,* Ishma's oldest child is a symbol of the strength of the mountains. Next pregnant with twins, she fights alone in the dead of night to drive a herd of cows from a thriving bean field that she and Britt have planted. The crop is destroyed, although Ishma admits that she knows the lead cow was only doing her job—finding food for her babies and her herd. The twins are born, but they die from croup when Britt and Ishma are away tending to the sick in other households. After this tragedy their marriage seems to crumble rapidly.

Dargan links the fertility of the mountain land and of Ishma's relationship with Britt to the fertility and productivity of the soil they farm. When Ishma leaves the mountains, she is pregnant with their fourth child, who at age three is hit by a car and killed. In the city, Ishma learns of birth control methods that allow her to control her own reproductive system. Despite the number of her pregnancies, though, and her nurturing nature, Ishma struggles with her maternity and for much of the book she seems to fail to recognize the contributions she makes as a nurturer. It is, however, her maternal instinct that ultimately directs her to help improve the mill workers' living conditions. By the end of the novel Ishma seems to feel complete as she hopes to nurture the mill workers and their children back to physical and emotional health. In particular, she speaks with Britt about raising chickens and cows to provide eggs and milk for the mill workers and their families. As nurturer, she will depend on the reproductive abilities of the female livestock and chickens.

For Janie, in *Their Eyes Were Watching God*, children never become an issue. When her grandmother hopes soon after Janie's marriage that she might be pregnant, Janie tells her, "No'm, Ah don't think so anyhow" (21). This is the only point in the novel when there is ever any mention of the possibility of Janie's being pregnant. Hurston allows Janie the chance to discover selfhood not through the role of mother but through marital relationships that might have the opportunity for equality. Janie is not tied to the home because of children. Whether Janie practiced birth control or was unable to have children, we never know. But Hurston seems to have made a decision to allow her character to explore life without the traditional womanly obligations that come from intimate relationships.

Woven through literature written by southern women in the 1930s are clear attempts by the authors to refocus women's lives, to allow for individuality that earlier seemed lacking for southern women. A trained anthropologist, Hurston was attempting in *Their Eyes Were Watching God,* as she did in a number of her writings, to preserve an African American folk tradition that she saw rapidly fading. *Their Eyes Were Watching God* is a complex of storytelling and yarns, a tribute to the oral tradition of the folk. But like *Gone with the Wind* and *Call Home the Heart, Their Eyes Were Watching God* is also the story of a woman journeying beyond the home place, leaving bonds of traditions that limited her to those boundaries.

Dargan obviously takes a political stand in *Call Home the Heart.* She, like fellow southerners Grace Lumpkin and Myra Page, wrote books about the mill strike in Gastonia, North Carolina, in spring 1929. The strike was also the inspiration for a number of other novels, including one by Sherwood Anderson. What made this strike different was the prominent role women played in it. Women mill workers were particularly concerned with the working conditions of the laborers at the mills. Working long hours and into the night, women workers had little time to care for their own families. Children were employed in the mills and had little chance to attend school. Workers were poorly paid, poorly fed and clothed, and susceptible to disease (Hapke 146–77). Laura Hapke explains that the mill women involved in the strike were not seeking to define themselves, to aspire individually, or to cross boundaries between the races. But the strike became the inspiration for six pro-labor novels because white women gathered together to fight the oppression of the working class (152).

Although Dargan's novel was intended to support the communist movement, the book ends with Ishma returning to the mountains and leaving behind the labor movement in the city. Although she will continue her efforts to help the mill workers, her efforts will be to provide these people with a place to commune with Nature, to find refreshment from their lives. In his essay in *The History of Southern Literature,* James Mellard writes that for Dargan, as well as for Myra Page and Grace Lumpkin, "the traditional values—the agrarian ideals of independence, hard work, and the land—ultimately triumphed over the more transient political ones" (354). *Call Home the Heart* actually received a good deal of criticism from communists who believed that the book did not fulfill the potential Dargan had hoped for it, so Dargan wrote a sequel that returns Ishma to the city and to the labor movement.

In *Their Eyes Were Watching God*, life "on the muck" brings with it an equality in marriage that Janie had not before experienced. By harvesting the rows with Tea Cake, Janie ultimately fulfills her desire for a truly intense, passionate relationship. Although the two work as hired hands, it is as if the owners of the property do not exist. What seems of primary importance is that Janie harvests the earth. For, in fact, she only harvests when she and Tea Cake are on the muck. Janie must also deal with Tea Cake's attentions to another woman and with a beating from Tea Cake, but despite these hardships, this section of the book suggests Janie has now been fully immersed in a relationship that allows her to be herself. After Tea Cake's death, Janie returns to Eatonville and can plant the seeds she has saved. The seeds remind her of Tea Cake because "he was always planting things." She finds them on the kitchen shelf when she returns home from the funeral and, placing them in her breast pocket, she plans—now that she is home—"to plant them for remembrance" (182). She can now both sow and reap the harvests from the love she shared with Tea Cake, and as a result, Janie has been empowered with a new sense of identity that reinforces her feelings of self-worth and that gives her control over her own life.

Likewise, in *Gone with the Wind,* Scarlett's attachment to the red earth of Tara and her desire to preserve her sense of independence and individual sovereignty are key to her willingness to wage war against those who would take the land from her and her family: "Yes, Tara was worth fighting for, and she accepted simply and without question the fight. No one was going to get Tara away from her. No one was going to set her and her people adrift on the charity of relatives. She would hold Tara, if she had to break the back of every person on it" (428). With that struggle, Scarlett reshapes her identify from southern belle to steel magnolia. Elizabeth Harrison also notes that Scarlett is neither "passive southern lady" nor "genteel aristocrat." *Gone with the Wind,* according to Harrison, is the American success story from a southern point of view, and the novel is actually a "paradoxical combination of southern pride and national patriotism." The daughter of a man who came to America with only the clothes on his back, Scarlett will "deal with anyone who strikes a good bargain, whether Yankee or cracker, thereby violating the southern chivalric code and threatening class hierarchy," writes Harrison (46). Ultimately, though, according to Harrison, *Gone with the Wind* always remains a southern pastoral novel in which the land is represented as feminine, and Scarlett's return to Tara at the end of the novel "indicates her entrapment in the southern garden" (63). I would argue, however, that Scarlett decides to return of her own free will because of the bond she has with the land. By the end of *Gone with the Wind*, Scarlett is in many ways like Hurston's Janie who has grown through her attachment to the earth and through her recognition of the creative nature that she contains and sustains as a woman.

Dargan's *Call Home the Heart* makes the most interesting and dramatic statement about the freeing role of Nature in the evolving lives of southern women. Dargan describes Ishma as possessing a special tie to the land, one that she cannot fully understand but one that continually draws her home. When she and Britt plant a bean field that is the envy of the neighbors because of its lushness, their marriage seems strong and vital. The crop is tied to their very beings; as Dargan explains, "It was part of themselves—that green abundance—flowing out of their bodies" (101). When a herd of cattle invades the field one night and destroys the crop despite Ishma's struggles to drive them away, Ishma and Britt are left hopeless. They had poured all their strength into planting and raising the crop, and now they have nothing. Crude food, no clothing—only "debts, sneers, injustice." "Nothing for study—books—trips. Just bare life" (106). Ishma can only see the barrenness of this life, and she is left in despair.

Dargan writes that as a child, Ishma "had rested sanely on her love of beauty in nature, and her unthinking union with it." She seemed to be free to move within Nature, within "that roominess of personal being": "A leaf in the dawn, glittering on its twig, belonged to her as much as her shaken, clinging curls. A glance upward at an amiable, drifting cloud could ease a growing irritation within her, and sometimes her sense of grace would not abandon her for a whole day. A storm on Cloudy Knob would leave her feeling that she had taken a breath as deep as her being. Wind, curving about a ridge of silver poplars, could sweep life clean." But as an adolescent, Ishma had come to believe that "beauty was not enough" because Nature left her "lonely, hungry, impatient." She was tormented by "an inquisitive denial of sensuous adequacy." With Britt, she feels restored and complete, and in the first few months of marriage, Ishma experiences the full joy of love and a full emotional and physical attachment to another human being. As the newness of the relationship seems to fade, Ishma sees life only as empty and barren. Ishma is torn between this perception of life and the people around her whom she knows she must nurture and care for, that is, Britt, their son Ned, and another child who is on the way. Dargan points out, though, that Ishma does not realize that for someone searching, questing in life, that love and beauty can be little more than "little nests for the comfort of the senses." She identifies the source of her sorrows as the need for "clean sheets and a sweet-smelling door," but Dargan explains that Ishma actually misidentifies the true "source of her suffering" (149–50).

Ishma is drawn to Britt because he represents the security of home in the mountains, and the physical attraction is a powerful one. When Britt returns from working a job far from home, Ishma and Ned greet him with the fullest of emotions. They had walked halfway to Beebread in order to greet him, and when they meet, she and Britt "kiss with abandon." The moment is an intimate one even though they are on the road, and no one sees them kiss and laugh—something that couples married for three years do not do. Britt also wishes to build his family a home by cutting logs for the house from the forest. Increasingly, Britt is tied to the mountains as he collects the materials for their home and eventually builds it. His music—his creative abilities, in particular—further ties him to the mountain land and its people. Although Britt becomes a creator, Ishma rejects her own abilities by fleeing her children and her home in the mountains and her ability to create children. Ultimately, though, she seems to accept that creative role when she becomes a nurturer, caring for those in need in the city and eventually hoping to invite mill workers and their families to the mountains for rest and recuperation.

But life for Ishma means more than what she has with Britt in the mountains. "She'd have to get out. Get to work that *meant* something" (199). Even when she leaves Britt for life in the city with Rad, Ishma is continually drawn to the natural world. Listening to Dr. Unthank, she hears instead Britt's voice and is compelled to search for woodland, reach the woods to stop the anguish that fills her. "If she could get to the woods!" she might find relief. She becomes "an uncontrollable channel for agony." Despite the benefits of life with Rad in the city, she misses the independence she had in the mountains. "It seemed to her that his presence enveloped the earth. There was no roof, no ground, no sky—just Rad between her and every thought and glimpse of life" (182–83). Life with Rad seems as limiting as marriage was with Britt. The town offers knowledge—information about birth control methods and books from the library—but still it gives her no relief from her "incessant inner questionings." Instead, she seeks the fields, always sure to return home early enough to prepare "an attractive supper" for Rad.

Ishma associates her life in the mountains with continued pregnancies, with ties to children she loves but who also represent bonds she would like to leave behind. After she gives birth to Vennie in the city, Ishma continues to feel bound and unproductive. Asking herself, "What did Vennie matter?" Ishma questions, "Was her life to be forever bound up in a child's? Was her horizon always to be Vennie's horizon? Was she never to reach the world?" (231). Ishma believes she has more to offer to humanity than being a mother, that she can help to bring about change in the lives of people beyond her family who might need her help.

For the mountain people who live in the city, choices are conflicted. Ishma's friend Cindy, who has known Ishma since childhood, sees the city as a place where she can finally have a bed; in the mountains it didn't matter if she slept on a pallet on the floor because she could sleep there. In the city, she might have a refrigerator, but she explains to Ishma that a refrigerator is a necessity for a mountain person because in the summer, a mountain person cannot drink water in the city without cooling it first. Ella Ramsey explains to Ishma that when she and her husband were farmers, they were able to raise enough to provide for their large family of children, but there are more "hungers than the one gnawin' yer stomach . . . There's more to life than a belly, an' we had to go to the mills for money." Her family leaves the city and millwork each time a new baby is on the way, but they return to the mill as soon as they can (224–25). Ella's story seems further proof to Ishma that the land offers little for her people.

Ishma gradually recognizes the freedoms that come with rural life. Feeling as if she might choke to death in the house in the city one warm day, she looks at the meal she has just cooked on the hot kitchen stove. She had cooked other meals with no stove at all. She thinks, too, of the mountain views she had when she cooked those meals—views of clouds on the mountains rather than of overstuffed furniture in a house. In the mountains, people did not judge others by what they had in their houses, Ishma remembers. "The neighbors wouldn't slant their eyes at you and make you hang your head" (219). In Winbury, people shut their windows to the rain and wind, fleeing from the elements of nature rather than living in them. When a person dies in the city, someone is paid to prepare the body for burial and to dig the grave. Even in the most intimate of life and death experiences, the impersonal ways of the city intrude and take away the comforts of community that Ishma knew to be at the heart of her life in the mountains.

Here, Dargan seems to be preparing the reader for Vennie's death, which immediately follows Ishma's observations about the most important of human rituals that are completed by strangers in the city. In search of natural surroundings where she can seemingly merge with the mother figure of Nature, Ishma seems lost in her contemplations as Vennie plays in the street by the park. Hit by a car (an obvious reference to the mechanization of city life), Vennie dies immediately, and Ishma, who comes to her senses long enough to try to save her daughter, is injured and taken to the hospital. Ishma decides that Vennie's body must be returned to the mountains to Britt and for burial. Ishma is now left without the complications of a child to tend, but she is also dealing with the injuries she suffers as a result of the accident. With another tie to her mountains severed, Ishma becomes increasingly involved in the labor movement, and the communist musings of the text become more prevalent.

Communal responsibility becomes a particularly prominent ideal in the text, and one comrade even suggests the roots of the mountain people support and inform communal living. He explains in a speech that his listeners need go back no further than a generation or two to find stories of their pioneer ancestors facing the wilderness. These pioneers traveled in groups, never thinking that they might take their wives and children into the wilderness on their own. These pioneers, "all brave men," worked together to build houses, dig wells, build fences. They would not have allowed other families to go without shelter or provisions because "every man was as much the protector of every other man's wife and child as of his own." Describing the present world as an even greater wilderness than that of their ancestors, the comrade suggests the even greater need for the mill workers to work together, to unite to battle and conquer the present-day wilderness. "There is but one road of survival for the human race," he says. "It must come out of the competitive jungle where it is swamped, and where nine-tenths of mankind are fighting for breath. It must find the firm and fertile ground of co-operation—of working together. There the house of life must be built if it is to stand. And it is we, the workers of the world, who must lead the way out, who must find that ground, who must build that house . . . " (285–86).

One farmer who offers Ishma a glimpse of the possibilities of co-operation is Abraham Beasley. Although he and his wife struggled through hardships to build a farm of a thousand acres, their children are not interested in continuing their parents' work. Beasley feels strongly about contributing his property to the communist effort, but he recognizes that traditional farming practices are not the answer. Farmers can not go back to "the days of Adam," says Beasley, "while the rest o' the world rolls along into the twenty-first century." "The first age of man" cannot be teamed up with the last, without "tangle and trouble." With a name like Abraham, this farmer surely gives an important insight when he says, "We've got to pool our farms, our tools, our labor, same as in any modern industry. We've got to let go before we can get a holt." A new system will both provide for those in old age and offer opportunity for the young (345–46).

When Ishma decides to return home, she first makes sure that

Rad will be cared for by another woman—a new love interest for him. Although Dr. Unthank believes Ishma is "surrendering, running away" (293), Ishma tells Britt, "I got to craving a sight of the mountains. Craving till I couldn't bear it" (399). When she starts home, she realizes she is on the right road, headed in the right direction. When she arrives, she sees it has "an air, not of plenty, but enough" (390). Britt, she finds, has been to New York where he was pursuing his musical talents. Ultimately, though, Britt found that he might be successful, but primarily because of his good looks rather than for his musical abilities. He did not want to be labeled as "a freak o' the wilderness" and decided to return home. Like Ishma, he has pursued a life beyond the mountains but has made the decision to return, and in this recognition, all she can think about is that Britt was "her own man." She had chosen to marry him, to stand beside him in her gingham dress and borrowed shoes because "love was the only thing in life that mattered" (403–4). Then, immediately, Ned appears—a reminder of a part of herself that she has left behind.

Ishma is drawn back to the mountains in part because she has read in the newspapers of the fires burning across the landscape, and she wants to see them for herself. When she sees the fire burning in the mountaintops, she feels herself become "fire, power, beauty." She is mesmerized by the fire, on the one hand considering jumping in, but on the other feeling that she must continue her work with the mill people with "power and fire" (424). Believing that she is about to jump into the fire when she only intends to jump to a path below that leads to Siler's Cove, Britt physically holds her back. He reminds her that the fire is hard on the young birds, and that the green laurel will be burned to a white so that its branches are like "tangled bones warping in the sun" (423). Ultimately, the two can express their enduring love. Britt does not plan to marry Julie, and Ishma says to Britt, "I lied when I said I didn't come back for you. That was all I was thinking about. Just getting to you" (428).

But Ishma knows, too, that she cannot forget the world beyond. She cannot run away into the past. She recognizes that the plow itself will be a thing of the past in just a matter of a few generations. And with this recognition, she sees, too, how she might help by leashing

Britt, "sturdy, beautiful, her golden primitive," to "the new age." Her plan, she says, will take a lot of milk and eggs, for she hopes to bring the mill children and their parents to the mountains each summer. She would "like to give them plenty to eat and turn them loose on the mountain to get strong." The families could live in bark shelters or old tobacco sheds, and some of the mothers could help Ishma with the hens and cows. Although she states clearly that she will leave the decision to Britt because the farm is his, she says that the mill workers would be "crazy to come and help" on the farm. Britt recognizes once again Ishma's maternal spirit, her willingness and urge to nurture, despite her desire to flee the bonds of motherhood. She only hopes that she might be able to give the children courage and a knowledge that Derry Unthank says the children must have. In the closing passage of the book, Ishma bends over to kiss Britt's forehead with "a protective kiss," but Dargan also reminds her readers that "A cup, though full, is not the sea" (432).

Although *Call Home the Heart* does, as a whole, achieve success as a book valuing the contributions of the labor movement for the betterment of southern society, communist readers criticized it as not following through with the important communist message. Likewise, in *From Tobacco Road to Route 66* (1976), Sylvia Jenkins Cook sees similar flaws in the book's ending. First examining a section of the novel in which Ishma is repelled by and strikes a black woman who is the wife of a union leader Ishma saved from a lynch mob, Cook points out that despite Ishma's growth over the course of the story, by the end of the novel she retreats to the mountains because of her racism. Ishma may have sacrificed throughout the book for an "intellectual integrity" that is ultimately betrayed in this act. According to Cook, the novel ends with a "joyous celebration of mountain and marriage" and a retreat into a "Jeffersonian idyll." But this ending and its "pristine enthusiasm" have been "distilled by the act of rejecting humanity for one human being" (107). In returning home, Cook believes, Ishma isolates herself from the outside world and rejects her responsibility to help change that world for the better.

If we read Ishma's return home as a result of her limited aspirations or because of flaws in her character that leave her unenlightened or passive, however, then Scarlett and Janie have also failed. In reality, though, they have not. All three of these women characters make strides in moving away from traditional images of southern womanhood. Despite Cook's claim, Ishma actually reclaims what she has pushed aside because she has finally discovered her role in the communist movement and thus her responsibility to the larger world. Ishma does not represent an ideal, but instead a person who is making strides to see beyond the limitations of the world that has shaped her. Her return to the mountains should be read not as a retreat but as a return. The same should be claimed for Janie and for Scarlett.

Such a return suggests a similar pattern in a number of southern writings by male authors which show a character's movement out into the world and an ultimate return home to emphasize the importance of accepting roots and attachments to place. Oftentimes, too, that return was a difficult one. In these stories of escape and return, male characters such as Robert Penn Warren's Jack Burden in *All the King's Men* and William Faulkner's Quentin Compson in *Absalom, Absalom!* struggle both with their desire to flee the South and with their urge to return (or perhaps retreat) to the region. Both Jack and Quentin attempt to win interior battles—one that leaves Jack at the end of *All the King's Men* with an awareness that he must carry the burden of the southern past with him, and the other that leads to Quentin's drowning in that past.

In many ways, however, this was a new narrative strategy for women writers like Hurston, Dargan, and Mitchell, who broke from a literary tradition that typically limited female characters to a domestic realm and often to the roles of belle, southern matron, and mammy. In a real sense, then, this draw to the soil—as tiller and as harvester—suggests a new freedom for southern women, one that proclaims women's budding sense of independence and assertiveness and their desire to reframe both their intellectual and their social beings. Because of the work of writers like Hurston, Dargan, and Mitchell, it is a freedom that women writers of the contemporary South have been able to savor.

6 Reinventing Faulkner

Although American myths of democracy played a major role in the literature of the twentieth-century South, many southern writers continued to be influenced by the myth of the plantation. The idea of democracy in southern literature is prominent but certainly not all encompassing.

William Faulkner is a case in point. He is part of this mix not only because of the American myths that play a role in his Yoknapatawpha saga but also because of what the scholarship about his writings tells us about the influence of myth-making in the field of southern literary studies. By continuing to define a body of literature as southern, and as set apart from other literatures, those who write about the South and those who read those texts ensure that the South and southern literature will remain distinct. History may say that the South will not rise again, but surely the South has re-created itself in literature, both creative and interpretive. In some cases, that re-creation has been an effort to change a southerner's perception of self and community. In others, it has meant revising the story of the South's past—for better or for worse.

Such a relationship between literary and interpretive traditions emphasizes the profound role that literary scholars have also played in shaping southern literary tradition. Southern literary history is full of examples of the ways that southern writers have created and shaped a mythology for a place we call the South. So, too, is the field of southern literary studies. The reader does not need to go far to find discussions that link southern literature with the literary scholars who study that literature. In his book *The Idea of the American South* (1979), Michael O'Brien reminds us of the far-ranging influence of Allen Tate and John Crowe Ransom, both Agrarians and New Critics. More recently, Michael Kreyling, in *Inventing Southern Literature*, describes southern literature as "an amalgam of literary history, interpretive traditions, and a canon." According to Kreyling, we—as creative authors, scholars, and readers—have invented and reinvented southern literature in our attempts at "keeping history at bay" (ix–xii). Kreyling claims that some of the most prominent scholars in southern literary studies, including Louis D. Rubin and Cleanth Brooks, have tended to read southern literature as "an untroubled rendition of the 'facts' of southern life." Rubin, Kreyling argues, "sees historical continuity as nonproblematical, seamless, untroubled by 'forgetting,' and immune from vexing questions of gender, sexuality, race, and class." Kreyling examines how the "orthodox narrative of identity" created by the New Critics and Rubin and Brooks has left a cloud over the field of southern literary studies, a case of "amnesia" that has left present-day scholars with a sense that "southern literature will always be recognizable by a formula as constant as the thing itself" because the South and the history of the South are "'facts' and 'entities' that remain intact in and impervious to literary representation" (xi–xii). In part, the argument of this book as a whole builds upon the work of scholars like Kreyling who see the study of southern literature as largely shaped by the politics of literary scholars.

One meaningful example of such reinventions can be found in the literary criticism concerned with Faulkner's imaginary Yoknapatawpha County. Interpreting Faulkner as a writer who upholds myths of democracy is an argument grounded more in critical analyses of his work rather than in the works themselves. Some literary scholars have interpreted Faulkner's writings so as to shadow over race issues and to set forth a reinterpretation of the South not quite so marred by the tragedies and complications that are generally associated with the region's racial heritage. Although this approach to Faulkner's work is certainly not representative, such readings point to the ways in which interpretative writings have been used to re-envision the South.

At the foundation of such readings lies the clear tension between the yeoman and planter traditions within Faulkner's life and works. Faulkner's fiction is often viewed in light of his life and the way he chose to portray himself. In his personal life, Faulkner clearly exemplified the conflict between farmer and planter. One of the most enduring images of Faulkner is of a gentlemanly sort dressed in a white suit and with pipe in hand, but Faulkner wrestled with the implications of that image. On his visit to Nagano, Japan, Faulkner explained in a conversation recorded there, "I'm a countryman, my life is farmland and horses and the raising of grain and feed . . . My life is a farmer" (*Faulkner at Nagano*, 142). Rowan Oak in Oxford, Mississippi, was a run-down farm in need of repair when Faulkner bought it, but like Andrew Jackson's Hermitage, the house at Rowan Oak was fronted by a line of white columns that represented a plantation South. Joseph Blotner, whose two-volume biography of Faulkner is perhaps the best known and most acclaimed, suggests that although some lookers-on might have judged Faulkner as having "styled" himself a farmer of his Greenfield farm property and created a persona about himself like "the maimed war hero and the bohemian poet," the avocation of farming was one that he worked at quite hard, if only for segmented periods of time (1395).

Faulkner's writings show a similar conflict between the planter and yeoman farmer. Jefferson, the county seat of Yoknapatawpha, represents the essence of that conflict. The name of the town is, of course, the name of the southern American statesman whose own agrarian ideals expressed the conflict between yeoman and cavalier, between farmer and planter. Although Faulkner tells us in *Requiem for a Nun* that the town was named for a federal mail rider of frontier Yoknapatawpha, critical interpretations range widely. Joseph R. Urgo argues "that Jefferson, Mississippi, is not named for Thomas Jefferson is critical . . . Faulkner's imaginary town does not represent or refer to the historical Thomas Jefferson, but to yet another fiction" (99–100). Peter Nicolaisen, by contrast, sees the naming of the community as part of "Faulkner's Dialogue with Thomas Jefferson." Pointing out that the people of Jefferson named their town for the Virginia statesman as a way to bribe Jefferson Pettigrew, the mail carrier, Nicolaisen describes the naming of the town as "an act of deceit." Pettigrew's mother named him after the Virginia statesman not as a tribute, but so that her son might have "some of his luck" (64). Nicolaisen points out that naming Flem Snopes's future town after Jefferson "must have appealed to the young author's sense of humor." He also reminds us that when Faulkner was asked years later at the University of Virginia about the naming of the town, Faulkner did not remember the details of the story he told in *Requiem for a Nun*. Pettigrew, according to Faulkner, "had been a *tenant* on Mr. Jefferson's place, one of Mr. Jefferson's places here in Albemarle County" (65). In effect, then, Faulkner's decision to name his town Jefferson seems ripe with many complications.

A look at Faulkner's map of Yoknapatawpha County also suggests ways in which the farmer and planter traditions diverge in his writings and the sharp contrasts between the peoples connected to those traditions. Frenchman's Bend, an area of Yoknapatawpha that is home primarily to farmers, and Sutpen's Hundred, a property that is the epitome of the plantation system, are located in opposite corners of Faulkner's map. These two places are actually wedged rather firmly into the map's corners, at equal distance from Jefferson, which lies at the heart of the county.

Although these tensions within Faulkner's writings suggest a struggle between yeoman and plantation Souths, his world is actually dominated by three groups of people—by southern planters, African Americans, and poor whites. He makes clear attempts to focus his Yoknapatawpha stories around these three groups in order to emphasize the power of southern myth-making that generally characterized southern culture as divided along lines of race and economics. Although the historical region of northern Mississippi was home to more farmers than planters, both farmers and planters also took part in myth-making that elevated their places in the community. As Myra Jehlen explains in *Class and Character in Faulkner's South,* farmers and planters saw one another as "a threat to survival." Fearing slave insurrections, the planters sometimes were fearful of what Jehlen refers to as "a redneck revolution." As a way to gain power over the other, farmers portrayed themselves as Jeffersonian yeomen, "upright tillers of the soil, the salt of the American earth." Planters, by contrast, laid claim to "classical ideas of order" as a means of gaining legitimacy for the feudal system they had created. They also believed that "only a leisure class" such as theirs "could attain the esthetic and ethical excellence to forward the course of civilization" (21). Faulkner inherited both of these traditions, but he was "unable fully to approve either one." Jehlen ultimately concludes that "This deference to a class whose way of life [Faulkner] considered ethically unwholesome, and the inverse, his inability to identify with the farmers, who, however abjectly, wore the yeoman's mantle, largely inspired [his] tragic vision of the South" (22–23).

On the one hand, Jehlen gets at the heart of a conflict within the life and writings of Faulkner. She argues that Faulkner frames a yeoman tradition grounded in myth rather than in reality. Note, in particular, that she describes these supposed yeoman farmers as "rednecks." Jehlen frames her central argument in her book around the aristocracy and the poor whites, and this seems to be the case in much of Faulkner criticism. Jehlen's reading of Faulkner's texts seems to be the generally accepted interpretation of Faulkner's county as a place of extremes. Yoknapatawpha County itself has been re-created by critics to show the myth-making of southern society and the attempts by southerners to reframe themselves within heroic traditions, whether those traditions be ones associated with chivalry or with the founding fathers and the founding of the United States.

Peter Nicolaisen's "William Faulkner's Dialogue with Thomas Jefferson," included in *Faulkner in America: Faulkner and Yoknapatawpha, 1998,* might, on the other hand, seem to lay claim to a yeoman tradition in Faulkner's writings. Nicolaisen's essay, however, is only a more contemporary reassertion of Jehlen's statements as he points out that Faulkner's "overall vision" in his created county is "a far cry from the agrarian order either Thomas Jefferson or his latter day disciples at Vanderbilt contemplated." Specifically pointing to the farmers of Frenchman's Bend, Nicolaisen makes a particularly strong case in the following passage:

When his country folk assert their independence, this often ends in violence or death . . . Most importantly, the economics of French-man's Bend go directly against the high hopes Jefferson entertained for a republic of independent farmers. The commodification, in *The Hamlet* and elsewhere, not only of the land, but of virtually every-thing, including the human body, the greed characteristic of nearly all of the male inhabitants of Yoknapatawpha, the lack of any sense of responsibility attached to the idea of ownership—all these leave little room for the stable, republican order Jefferson imagined. Such conditions pave the way for the rise of Flem Snopes, a figure Jef-ferson would no doubt have associated with the commercial world of Alexander Hamilton that he despised, not with that of a virtuous agrarian republic. (67)

Nicolaisen argues that although in the early 1940s, with the story "The Tall Men," Faulkner aligned himself with the Jeffersonian yeo-man, he actually did "much more outspokenly so than was his wont" (69). In Nicolaisen's estimation it is one of the later novels, *A Fable,* that best shows Faulkner's cynicism in regards to Jeffersonian de-mocracy. Nicolaisen describes Faulkner's characters in the novel who are "the people, by whom the author of the Declaration of Indepen-dence set such great store" as "sadly wanting—they are inarticulate, easily swayed, and have no idea who controls them" (78).

While Jehlen, Nicolaisen, and others have framed readings of Faulkner's Yoknapatawpha County that seem both typical and well reasoned, other literary scholars have interpreted Faulkner's writ-ings so that the yeoman farmer appears to have the primary role in Yoknapatawpha. One particularly meaningful example of this rein-vention of Faulkner is found within a group of interpretive essays published by M.E. Bradford and Elmo Howell during the 1960s and early 1970s. Bradford published his "Faulkner's 'Tall Men'" in 1962, "Faulkner and the Jeffersonian Dream: Nationalism in 'Two Soldiers' and 'Shall Not Perish'" in 1965, "Faulkner's 'Tomorrow' and the Plain People" in 1965, and "What We Can Know for Certain" in 1970. Elmo Howell's "William Faulkner and the Plain People of Yoknapatawpha County" came out in 1962. Both Bradford and Howell read Faulkner's writings within the context of the myth of the common man and woman, and their connections to American democracy. By framing Faulkner's writings in this way, by "reinventing" Faulkner so to speak, the issue of race in his writings becomes less charged and intense. While such a reading of Bradford's work is clear and strong, Howell takes part in a similar interpretation, although not to the same degree.

Nevertheless, these scholars' works signaled an attempt to revise the history Faulkner represented in his stories and novels of Yoknapatawpha so that Faulkner's people appear more democratic and yeoman-like. Written during the civil rights movement, these critical studies suggest an attempt to revise the history of the South during a period of great social upheaval and change. This type of scholarship imposes a reading of southern history that diverges from what Faulkner intended; it instead supports a view of the South that in the 1960s challenged contemporary characterizations of the region as a hotbed of racial injustice. By emphasizing the Americanness of Faulkner's writings, by claiming his world was a world of the yeoman, both Bradford and Howell promote a southern history not of degradation, not of guilt.

The civil rights movement had a decided impact on the course of southern literary history. Race and the history of racial oppression in the South came to the forefront in the works of southern writers during the 1960s and 1970s, and in many ways, the movement was instrumental in creating a contemporary southern literature that is now more racially and ethnically diverse. Rich, influential novels such as Margaret Walker's 1966 *Jubilee,* along with Alex Haley's *Roots* and Ernest Gaines's *The Autobiography of Miss Jane Pittman,* both published in the 1970s, recognized and reclaimed the African and African American pasts of the novels' characters. The years of the civil rights movement, however, also reflected in literature a sense of bitterness and of hopelessness in the midst of the struggles faced by blacks in the South. When Tucker Caliban in William Melvin Kelley's *dem* (1964), for example, destroys his southern farmland by spreading salt on the earth, he has, as the editors of *The Literature of the American South* suggest, "concluded that no hope, no possibility for a healthy future, exists in the South" (589).

While southern black writers were retrieving a past that recognized the significance of African roots and pointing to remaining racial inequalities, one white southern response was to cloud the issues of race. M. E. Bradford, for example, portrays Faulkner's writings within a perspective that reconfigures the writings from a context related to the southern planter to one framed by the American farmer. In effect, retelling the southern story serves as a means of shifting opinion about the South. In fact, though, such a reconstruction of Faulkner's writings is in clear correspondence with conservative ideology that figured so prominently in Mel Bradford's life and work. In his essay on Faulkner and Jefferson entitled "All the Precious Things," Mark Malvasi explains that southern conservatism has at its roots a dependence on the significance of property and the ideal of the farmer. Robert Beverley, for example, believed that owning and controlling property formed the very foundation of southern communities and the southern way of life. Southern thinker and American statesman Thomas Jefferson praised the farmer with almost sacred reverence, while John Taylor of Caroline held that it is only through farming that human beings are able to achieve worth and prosperity (133). Within the context of Faulkner's writings, Bradford would have us believe that "most of Faulkner's white male characters who are not Snopeses, Sartorises, or white trash" are yeoman farmers, that Faulkner's world is populated in large proportion by the yeomanry. Surely Bradford goes too far in his assessment, but in doing so, he argues for his own politics.

According to both Bradford and Howell, Faulkner's yeomen play a central role in the Yoknapatawpha saga. In "Faulkner's 'Tall Men,'" for example, Bradford spends much time discussing the McCallum family and explains that Faulkner's tall men "belong in spirit to the republic of independent farmers into which Thomas Jefferson had hoped the United States would develop" (30). Bradford also refers to the McCaslin brothers Buck and Buddy who in *The Unvanquished* live simply and treat their slaves as "charges, not things" (37). Bradford sees the McCaslins within this yeoman context, but he glosses over the fact that although the McCaslins do not live in a fine mansion, they own a fine mansion in decline, a vast acreage, and numerous slaves. In "Faulkner and the Jeffersonian Dream," Bradford creates a similar idealism. Explaining that Faulkner "goes beyond admiration to make [the Grier family] the ground for his most openly patriotic statement," Bradford says that in the stories about the Griers, Faulkner "aligns himself with the age-old Jeffersonian conception of the Republic which is still very much alive in the South, though now rarely voiced in such unequivocal terms" (94). As he does when he writes of the Griers, Bradford also points out in his "Faulkner's 'Tomorrow' and the Plain People" the neglect of the plain people or the yeoman farmer in literary criticism. In a similar fashion, Elmo Howell writes of Faulkner's plain people as overlooked and examines them within an American framework, explaining that the plain people are rooted in "the spirit of a time that is only a memory to urbanized, industrialized America" (73).

When Bradford begins to list other families that fit into the same category with the McCallums, his defining term becomes "plain folk." Among the characters he lists as part of the yeoman strain are Jackson Fentry in "Tomorrow," the Griers in "Shall Not Perish" and "Two Soldiers," Mr. Ernest in "Race at Morning," Byron Bunch in *Light in August,* the tall convict in "The Old Man," Mink Snopes in *The Mansion,* and the Bundren family in *As I Lay Dying.* The farmers of the Frenchman's Bend area, including the McCallums and the McCaslin twins who in reaction to their aristocratic background take up the life of the yeoman, are all situated on the east side of Yoknapatawpha, in the rising elevation of the hill country. The heart of the argument for both Bradford and Howell lies within the McCallum family, although they play a minor role in *Sartoris* and are the focus of only one story, "The Tall Men."

In *Sartoris* (1929), Faulkner contrasts the McCallum family with the Sartorises, who represent Old South aristocracy. The younger Bayard Sartoris of the novel is the epitome of the twentieth-century man full of anger at his inability to control his life in a world run into chaos. A veteran of World War I, he has lost his twin brother, John, to the war and blames himself for John's death. Only months after John's death, and before Bayard returns home, Bayard's wife and newborn son die in childbirth. When he returns home after the war, he is distraught, unable to function, besought with a desire to kill himself. He is the modern man behind the wheel of the modern machine, literally driving his car dangerously into the next curve in the road.

As boys, Bayard and John hunted foxes and coons with the Mc-Callums during vacations. Bayard connects the McCallums with the memories of his own past and an idealized period of his life. As a means of comforting himself, Bayard takes out some important mementoes of John's boyhood: "a garment, a small leather-bound book, a shotgun shell to which was attached by a bit of wire a withered bear's paw" (214). The bear's paw was from the first bear that John killed, and the shotgun shell is the remainder of the ammunition he used to kill it in the river bottom on the McCallums' farm. After Bayard's grandfather suffers a heart attack and dies in a car crash as he rides along trying to save Bayard from himself, Bayard finds refuge from the present at the McCallum home. Clearly, though, Bayard's journey to the McCallums is an escape. The family does not know that Bayard's grandfather is dead or the circumstances of his death—and Bayard does not tell them. Despite the fact that they mention the elder Bayard, wondering why he does not come to their home for a hunting trip and wishing him well, the younger Bayard holds back the truth—of his guilt and dishonor.

In sharp contrast to Bayard, the McCallums live their lives with honor. They are a people who are connected with their past. The elderly father, Virginius, remains the strong head of their home as he takes the only chair and his sons gather around him and their guest. Virginius, or Old Anse as he is known, is described as a "tall man," one who despite his age "tower[s] above his sons by a head" (314). He is "straight as an Indian," according to Faulkner, a description typical for Faulkner who, like Donald Davidson, equated tallness with strength and courage. There is a sense, too, that the tradition of the father's strength has been passed from parent to child, for Buddy, who has a "lean and fluid length," towers as high as his father, above the heads of his brothers (314).

Faulkner also describes the McCallum family as particularly in tune with nature. They are a masculine household, men, primarily, who farm the land, raise livestock, and hunt. As Bayard approaches their home, a tame fox appears and disappears under the house. Bayard later finds that the McCallums have mated the fox with one of their hunting dogs to produce a higher-grade tracker. The McCallums are so much in touch with the natural world that they are able to shape it and even improve upon it. And although Bayard is sure that the weather will not turn to rain, Virginius McCallum says that it will—and it does. The McCallums live close to the earth, and they know its inner workings.

They are a family strongly knit, unwilling to break the bonds among them. "With their dark, saturnine faces," they are "all stamped clearly from the same die" (315). Bayard's first view of Virginius is of a man silhouetted "against the clay fireback, swirling in wild plumes into the chimney's dark maw" as if his head is "haloed by the shaggy silver disorder of his hair" (309). The sitting room is described as "filled with warmth and a thin blue haze pungent with cooking odors" (316). It is hospitable and warm. Melvin Backman points to the significance of the hearth as a "refuge of warmth and light" to the younger Bayard (8). Verbal communication among them seems unnecessary because they share a "single thought." They are a family so tightly bound that they seem as one. Young Bayard's despondency, however, keeps him from the light of their hearth. As Backman explains, "Bayard's despair—described as cold, dark, savage, and bleak—cuts him off from the light and warmth and pulls him toward death" (9). In bed that night young Bayard is described as "shaking slowly and steadily with cold; beneath his hands his flesh was rough and without sensation; yet still it jerked and jerked as though something within the dead envelope of him strove to free itself" (323). Bradford comments that for Bayard, "now [the McCallums'] world offers him no solace, only sharpens his sense of guilt" (33).

The McCallums exist outside of time—they are not controlled by it. Their isolated home is tucked away in the woods, far from Jefferson. When Bayard enters their house of chinked logs, he notices the outdated calendars on the wall and the bare, hand-planked boards of the floor. The McCallums sharply contrast with a Faulkner character like Quentin Compson, who is obsessed with time and its passage. For the McCallums, time seems to stand still. On the one hand, they are idealized because they live in the past. But on the other hand, the values they epitomize are timeless and enduring. Living on land settled by their progenitors, the McCallums live their lives responsibly. They have pride in their family and care for themselves and their kin without outside help or intrusion. They retain the clannishness of their highlander ancestors and live close to the earth in the tradition of the Native Americans that Faulkner suggests have the most intimate and powerful relationship with the land. They are set apart from all else in the modern world—a suggestion that the modern world cannot destroy such idealism, but also a comment on their inability to live within the world, a world of perpetual change.

Such idealism, however limited, becomes the central argument for Bradford and Howell in formulating a Yoknapatawpha County that does not revolve around the taint of slavery and racism that many scholars read as a focal point of Faulkner's writings. Howell, for example, describes the McCallum home in *Sartoris* as the setting for "one of the most idyllic scenes in Faulkner" and "Faulkner's Utopia, a country of tall men with clean minds and pure hearts and nature still in a virginal state of innocence" (80). They live the "semi-arcadian life of the small farmer in northern Mississippi" (74). Likewise, Bradford's claim that "the world of the McCallums is Bayard's Paradise Lost" suggests a role for the yeoman farmer that seems to outweigh the significance of the numerous representations of black Southerners throughout Faulkner's entire body of work.

Both Bradford and Howell frame their literary studies of Faulkner's yeomen within an historical context. Both refer to Frederick Olmsted's descriptions of the South that led many northerners to believe that all white southerners could be categorized as either poor whites or aristocrats. They also refer to Frank Owsley's arguments that the majority of antebellum white southerners were farmers—not planters or poor whites. Bradford points out that "for some reason critics of Faulkner's fiction have generally ignored the role played in that fiction by these 'tall men.'" He states that he believes this "oversight" is a continuation of earlier misunderstandings that have shaped our interpretations of southern history and culture (30). In a similar fashion, Elmo Howell notes, "in the popular mind, the white man in Mississippi is either a planter or a 'poor white.'" Explaining that Faulkner's plain people are "neither very high nor very low," Howell calls them "a sturdy, simple race, whose long association with the earth has kept them faithful to the old way of doing things" (73). Bradford's opinions concerning the link between yeoman values and conservative ideology were summed up in the early 1970s when he wrote "What We Can Know for Certain: Frank Owsley and the Recovery of Southern History." A review of a 1969 edition of Owsley's essays, "What We Can Know" also sets forth Bradford's argument that "Unless [the yeomanry of the Old South] be hidden from view, the whole 'liberal' theory of American history is undone; unless their primary impact on Southern life (at least until after World War I) be cast in doubt, talk of 'totalitarian regimes' or 'slave power' can have no validity" (665). Bradford's statement suggests, then, that liberals—including scholars and historians—have attempted to misrepresent the yeoman farmer's significant role in southern history so as to forward their own agendas, which require representing southern culture as based on slavery.

Both Bradford and Howell try to explain the omission of the yeoman farmer in critical studies of Faulkner's writings by finding a reason within history—not within Faulkner's literary achievements. But Faulkner's imaginary county is just that—imaginary. Faulkner's map of Yoknapatawpha, including the populations of both black and white residents, makes this quite clear. Faulkner chose not to include a college in Jefferson, even though a major university is located in Oxford. He chose a higher number of African American citizens in the population of Yoknapatawpha than lived in Lafayette County in order to point to the persistent issues of race in the South. Clearly, Faulkner wanted to represent Yoknapatawpha County as a much more isolated locale than Lafayette County and one where the issues of race were more intensely felt. Although Frank Owsley's *Plain Folk of the Old South* suggests some essential truths about the nature of southern antebellum culture, both Bradford and Howell speak of Owsley's book as a truth that limits Faulkner's imaginative exploration of the American South. They both seem to ignore the fact that Faulkner's Yoknapatawpha is not real. Howell's essay was published in *The Journal of Mississippi History*—not in a literary journal, and it calls special attention to texts that show how southern literature has become part of the text of southern history. Likewise, southern literary criticism is intricately woven into the fabric of southern literary history.

Elizabeth Fox-Genovese and Eugene Genovese speak specifically to this issue in an essay included in *A Defender of Southern Conservatism: M. E. Bradford and His Achievements* (1999). "What [Bradford] and modern Southern conservatives wish to forget, however, and what their slaveholding forebears understood is that the social relations of slavery grounded the culture of the Old South" (81). "At bottom," they explain, "Bradford wanted the Old South to have been a yeoman society, with the planters viewed merely as a more successful version of the family farmer" (85). The Genoveses argue that while "the legacy of slavery and the burden with which it encumbers southern whites and blacks alike runs like a thread through most of Faulkner's work . . . at some level, Bradford knew as much, but, like many of Faulkner's protagonists, he did not always want to know." As a result, Bradford "effectively excised the memory of slavery from the South he sought to claim and preserve" (91). Bradford does so by focusing his scholarship on the yeoman farmer, by claiming a major significance for a figure that actually plays a small role in Faulkner's stories and novels.

"The Tall Men" is the perfect story to provide the focus for Bradford's argument because it is a story that concerns itself with American values and the necessity of southern support for American involvement in World War II. Like the stories of the Grier family that are set during World War II, "The Tall Men" shows the family's ties to a southern past of loyalty and honor, but it also emphasizes American patriotism. Written and published during World War II, "The Tall Men," along with two other Faulkner stories entitled "Two Soldiers" and "Shall Not Perish," honor the strong yeoman values that not only place the McCallum and Grier families within the framework of southern history but also move them into a significant place in fighting for the future of the United States.

"The Tall Men" shows not only the McCallum family's independence and their willingness to support their country but also their rejection of a system they believe is new-fangled and more complex than it needs to be. Howell claims for these young men an "old-fashioned patriotism" that the state draft investigator does not understand (82). Born into a modern world that seems to have little room for them, the present-day McCallums have inherited the strength, endurance, and independence of Old Anse. The McCallum twins, Anse and Lucius, "two absolutely identical blue-eyed youths" (49), are "the livin,' spittin' image of Old Anse McCallum. If Old Anse had just been about seventy-five years younger, the three of them might have been thriblets" (55). Farmers who studied a year at an agricultural college, they have also inherited the "tallness" of their grandfather. They seem unlike most young men of their day. The young men and their family cannot understand that the government now wants all young men to register for the draft, even though they are not yet being called into the service of the United States government, which is now facing the inevitability of entering the conflict of World War II. From the McCallums's perspective, young men should not need to be drafted to support their country. They should instead march willingly off to war to fight for their homeland.

Faulkner emphasizes their patriotism by telling the story of Old Anse. When the Civil War began, Anse McCallum, then about sixteen years old, walked all the way back to Virginia from his home in Mississippi to enlist. He could have enlisted in Mississippi and fought there, but his mother was a Carter, and his roots were in Virginia, "so wouldn't nothing do him but to go all the way back to Virginia to do his fighting." He had never been to Virginia, but he walked all the way there to fight for her. He enlisted in Stonewall Jackson's army, "stayed in it all through the Valley, and right up to Chancellorsville, where them Carolina boys shot Jackson by mistake, and right on up to that morning in 'Sixty-five when Sheridan's cavalry blocked the road from Appomattox to the Valley" (54). After the war Anse walked back to Mississippi, married, and built a home for his family. Old Anse had a loyalty to his homeland, courage to fight in battle, and an honor that guided him.

Because the young McCallums have not registered for the draft, Mr. Pearson, a young state draft investigator, accompanied by the old deputy marshal, Mr. Gombault, has been sent to arrest the twins as evaders. Pearson is disturbed when he finds that the marshal called ahead to tell the McCallums they were coming. But the marshal explains that since they left Jefferson he has been trying to tell Pearson something he should not forget. "I reckon it will take these McCallums to impress that on you," he adds (46). Pearson sees the marshal as a "doddering, tobacco-chewing old man" whose office should give him a character of "honor and pride" (46). Pearson believes the McCallums lie to "honest" people in government jobs. He equates them with freeloaders who lie and cheat for relief jobs, a government-subsidized mattress, free food or housing, or a seed loan. He cannot understand why, when the United States is threatened by external forces, people who have received so much from the government will not even put down their names on a piece of paper. Registering—"that's all required of them" (50).

What Pearson does not understand is that the McCallums have passed down through the generations a sense of responsibility and honor and pride. The young men listen carefully to their father, Buddy, and answer him "as one" (50) when he explains that he would like them to enlist in his old infantry. Buddy served in World War I, where he was awarded two medals: one from the American government and another from the French. Telling them that they should obey their commanding officers until they know how to be soldiers, he adds, "remember your name and don't take nothing from no man" (53). Despite the objections of the investigator that the young men should follow proper procedures, the twins kiss their father and then leave to enlist, not bothering to answer the charges against them in Jefferson.

Essentially, Faulkner reframes this southern family to suggest the ways its members have become, and must continue to become, Americans. Faulkner, in effect, redefines them as Americans, not southerners. Old Anse reminded his boys about his journey to Virginia to fight for her; Buddy now reminds his sons of his own service to America and builds a new legacy in the family of service to the country at large. Faulkner clearly links the McCallums' sense of valor and honor to an American past and frames them within an American context.

At the McCallums' home, there is a proper place and order that does not exist for many of Faulkner's other families. Even in the midst of pain, the McCallums exemplify the best of qualities. Buddy catches his leg in the hammer mill as he works, but despite the great pain he is suffering, he takes responsibility for what has happened, acknowledging "Ah, it was my own damn fault" (49). He claims he doesn't need ether to knock him out while the doctor removes the leg: "I could whet up one of Jackson's butcher knives and finish it myself, with another drink or two" (51). After the surgery is complete, the marshal and the investigator bury the leg in the spot in the cemetery where Buddy will be buried some day. There is an order in the cemetery that will be followed as each family member is buried. At the root of the McCallum spirit is also an individualism that is particularly important to Faulkner. Modern life has made it difficult for human beings to hang on to that individualism and has increasingly made Americans subservient to the government. Government programs that pay citizens not to work have resulted in men without backbones and without the qualities of honor and pride. Old Anse left an inheritance to his descendents of honor and pride that they have carried on by working the fields, raising their crops, maintaining their lives. To use a phrase from Bradford (who nods to Glasgow), the McCallums have a "vein of iron"—an inheritance of endurance and strength.

Faulkner crafted a special role for the plain people or the yeoman farmers in his Yoknapatawpha County. In "The Tall Men," for example, Faulkner alludes to the same values that he describes in his Nobel Prize acceptance speech on "the old verities and truths of the heart": "the courage and honor and hope and pride and compassion and pity and sacrifice which have been the glory of [humanity's] past." Man is immortal, Faulkner said, and humanity will "endure and prevail" despite the travesties of the modern world because Man "has a soul, a spirit capable of compassion and sacrifice and endurance." The marshal preaches a lesson of values quite close to the qualities Faulkner validated in his Nobel Prize acceptance speech, but the marshal's words also clearly set him within a modern context, for he explains, "We done forgot about folks. Life has done got cheap, and life ain't cheap." But life should not be valued in monetary terms, he says. "Life's a pretty durn valuable thing. I don't mean just getting along from one WPA relief check to the next one, but honor and pride and discipline that make a man worth preserving, make him of any value" (60). The marshal points, in particular, to the fact that human struggles can lead human beings back to these values. Perhaps Old Anse learned the lesson from walking back to Virginia, from losing the war, and from walking home. He learned the lesson well enough that he passed it on to his sons and grandsons. The marshal, perhaps summing up Faulkner's attitude, at least as it meshes with the Nobel Prize speech, says to the investigator: "We have slipped our backbone; we have about decided a man don't need a backbone any more; to have one is old-fashioned. But the groove where the backbone used to be is still there, and the backbone has been kept alive, too, and someday we're going to slip back onto it. I don't know just when nor just how much of a wrench it will take to teach us, but someday" (59). Faulkner's story, however, is influenced by the times in which it was written. He seems eager to reposition his yeoman farmers because of the role that they play as soldiers who can fight for the American cause during World War II.

Bradford, on the other hand, seems intent on rewriting southern history by pointing to "The Tall Men." He recognizes in the McCallums a reflection of the Jeffersonian ideal of the yeoman farmer, and he takes up the same argument again in "Faulkner and the Jeffersonian Dream" in which he discusses the Grier family of "Shall Not Perish" and "Two Soldiers." "Faulkner and the Jeffersonian Dream," however, is as much an espousal of Bradford's own politics as it is an interpretation of Faulkner's writings. In "Shall Not Perish," both Mrs. Grier and Major DeSpain have lost sons in World War II. When the Griers visit Major DeSpain's mansion to acknowledge their shared grief, Major DeSpain responds by saying that his son "had no country . . . His country and mine both was ravaged and polluted and destroyed eighty years ago." Bradford first refers to DeSpain's words and then quotes Thomas Jefferson, saying that DeSpain and his ancestors saw no worth in a society in which "dependence begets subservience and venality, suffocates the germ of virtue and prepares fit tools for the designs of ambition." Mrs. Grier's answer, according to Bradford an answer that is a reflection of the lives of the yeoman farmers, is "that the old Republic is not dead, that the anthill of contemporary American life is a passing phenomenon, a temporary falling away from 'the old verities,' that the nation's people are yet 'capable of courage and honor and sacrifice,' qualities which Faulkner's yeomen act out in their unheralded lives." Although Mrs. Grier believes that Americans will ultimately be able to retrieve those values and strengths of the past, she knows it will take time and experience and loss. According to Bradford, Mrs. Grier "implies" that "Wars fought to preserve freedom and 'independence' will . . . make men more aware of the importance of both to a meaningful life and of the earning, the sweat and blood required of men who would preserve them." She has come to recognize, with the deaths of her own son and Major DeSpain's son, that the trials of World War II will "recall the United States to something of its forsaken destiny" (97). Mrs. Grier "implies," according to Bradford, a message straight from Jefferson.

Bradford continues his argument with the McCaslin twins of *The Unvanquished,* whom he describes as similar to the Griers in the yeoman-like qualities they represent. Uncle Buck and Uncle Buddy McCaslin, according to Bradford, "repudiate their father's ruthless ways" ("Faulkner's 'Tall Men'" 36). Sons of a "Sutpen-like autocrat" named Carothers McCaslin, the McCaslin brothers live in a cabin rather than in the unfinished mansion that their father began to build. Bradford points out that the brothers live in a "simple two-room cabin with a dog-run, just like the house built by Anse McCallum in 1866" (37). The design of their cabin, however, is not particularly significant—it was in the style typical of the times. They may treat their slaves "as charges, not things," as Bradford says, but the brothers continue to hold their slaves in bondage. "Knowing that the Book says that the sins of the father shall descend to the generations of his sons," says Bradford, they "take the responsibility for what Carothers has done" (37). Although Bradford argues that the brothers differ from Ike McCaslin who withdraws from responsibility, in effect, the brothers only reframe their responsibilities. They remain patriarchs, holding people they believe to be lesser human beings, remaining slaveholders and continuing the sins of the fathers.

Claiming that the McCaslin brothers form a sort of "co-opera-tive agricultural enterprise," Bradford explains that "like patriarchs of old," the McCaslins see to the well-being of both black and poor white of their region (37). Attempting to purify them, he suggests the twins have not a "private" design like a Thomas Sutpen. Instead, they "seek no more than they need for themselves." Although he points to their yeoman dress, home, way of life, and "habits of mind," they are patriarchs who "must keep control over large numbers of people and a vast acreage if they are to fulfill their responsibilities" (37–38). The heart of Bradford's argument is that the McCaslins are different from the Sutpens, the Compsons, the De Spains, and their own fa-ther because "they believed that the land did not belong to people but the people belonged to the land" (38). Bradford's argument, though, seems weakened by his inclusion of the McCaslins. Surely a belief needs to be lived. Surely a patriarch with a "vast acreage" and "control over large numbers of people" is a planter—not Jefferson's farmer.

Clearly, Faulkner emphasizes admirable qualities possessed by families like the McCaslins, the Griers, and the McCallums. They uphold traditions and ideals that are at the heart of what he values most. In the end, had Faulkner really wanted to promote the yeo-man, then he could have. He does, in fact, portray the McCallums very idealistically, but as Bradford admits, Faulkner's worldview is es-sentially a tragic one. Although his yeoman characters are admirable ones, making too much of their significance calls attention away from the central issues of his writings. Faulkner himself seemed to have in mind the necessity of portraying southern families such as the McCallums and the Griers as upholding American ideals during the world wars. Perhaps, though, it is understandable that by the 1960s, scholars were reading Faulkner's stories in the context of the racial issues faced by the South.

Yeomen or small farmers play a limited role in Faulkner's world. Although Bradford may claim that in the yeoman farmer, Faulkner found "a usable past, a tradition among his people with which he can measure other traditions, southern or otherwise," that measuring stick does not reach far. The "tall men" of Faulkner's stories, according to Bradford, offer "a moral alternative to both the withdrawn passivity and sense of hopelessness and the aggressive, empire-building will-to-power which animate most of [Faulkner's other] characters" (39). But what sort of "moral alternative" is this if it does not rear its head very high? Instead, Bradford seems to have discovered his own usable past—the one he hoped to perpetuate.

7 "Leave the Rest Behind"

SOUTHERN AMERICAN MIGRANTS AND THE HEROIC PLOW

As Ellen Chesser looks back at her life near the conclusion of Elizabeth Madox Roberts's 1926 novel *The Time of Man*, Roberts describes Ellen's life as one defined by the literal and figurative roads that she travels: "Life began somewhere on the roads, traveling after the wagons where she had claim upon all the land and no claim, all at once, and where what she knew of the world and what she wanted of it sparkled and glittered and ran forward quickly as if it would always find something better. Down one road and up another and down again" (381–82).

The daughter of a tenant farmer who followed the road to jobs farming other men's fields, Ellen marries Jasper Kent who lives in much the same way as her father, Henry. While the book is set in the Knobs country of Kentucky at the turn of the century, Henry has led a life that has led him "all the way to Tennessee then on to Georgia and back once and on to Tennessee once again" (177). Although Henry speaks of his unwillingness to put down roots, to become tied to a specific plot of land, Jasper is in search of a place to settle, good land to raise a crop and a family. Ellen recollects "it had seemed forever that she had traveled up and down roads." At once broken down and strengthened by laboring in the fields, she knows the animals of the road—horses and dogs—rather than those of settlement, such as cows. She associates her own migrations with her inability to lay claim to the land. All that she can have is what she "snatched as she passed" (381).

The goal of a settled life on a plot of land Ellen's family can call their own always seems elusive. As she moves from one farm to the next, from one tenant house to another, Ellen always dreams about the possibilities of their next home—that it will be closer to the rich soil and have a well-maintained farmhouse. At each place they stop, she tries to raise a garden and livestock to help sustain her family. She hopes to create a home that provides comfort and life-giving sustenance. Imagining the place they will go to next, she thinks about the "Good land lying out smooth, a little clump of woodland, just enough to shade the cows at noon, a house fixed, the roof mended, a porch to sit on when the labor was done . . . a house on a green hill, a well with a bright new pump, the handle easy to lift, the water coolly flowing" (327). The roads lead to new possibilities, but they also suggest the inevitability of an endless journey.

Joseph R. Urgo fashions a particularly interesting and useful thesis for studying Roberts's novel, and American literature in general, when he explains in his book *Willa Cather and the Myth of American Migration* (1995) that while we typically think of American regional literature as grounded in distinct places, in fact, American life is actually based in patterns of migration, patterns of movement. Urgo claims that although the "sense of place," the "tremendous sense of loss," and places like Faulkner's "little postage stamp of native soil" are "the meat and potatoes of American literature," "Americans keep moving, accumulating hometowns like military campaign medals." The American experience has been shaped by migration, not only as the first Native Americans made their way into the Americas after crossing the northwest passage from Asia and as the first Europeans reached the eastern seaboard and then moved westward, but also in contemporary life as Americans move in search of better jobs and living conditions. "The picture of life in the United States is a moving picture," according to Urgo. "Our sense of community is in transit; the consciousness we share is migratory" (13). Urgo also suggests that historians and literary scholars who have moved away from their home places (their own "little postage stamps of native soil") have actually perpetuated the myths of place and origin in their studies of American history and literature, thereby de-emphasizing the significance of migration in American culture and labeling migration as an "aberrant or marginal" experience (4).

American literary history is shaped by what Urgo calls the "dialectic between migration and settlement," a relationship that is at the core of New World history. In the nineteenth century, the writings of Hawthorne and Melville suggest this dialectic, especially with Hawthorne's house and Melville's ship. Likewise, Frederick Douglass in his *Narrative* writes of the tension between the desires of many slaves to at once escape slavery and remain connected with their family homes in the South. The conflict between migration and settlement also seems particularly apparent when Mark Twain's Huckleberry Finn laments "it was rough living in the house all the time," while later he finds that "there warn't no home like a raft, after all" (1–2).

Although Urgo focuses on Virginia-born Willa Cather in his study, he makes some powerful observations that help us think about the role of migration in American literature and its relationship to the ideal of the farmer in southern literature. At the beginning of the first Southern Renaissance more and more southerners were moving beyond the literal and figurative boundaries of the South and reflecting on the relationship between the southern past and the present of the early twentieth century. According to the *Encyclopedia of Southern Culture,* "the South has historically exported its people by the millions" (1401). From the end of the nineteenth century until present times, tremendous numbers of southerners have either left the South or moved within the South in search of better job opportunities and living conditions. During the first decades of the twentieth century, depressed conditions in the Upper South led families like Ellen Chesser's to move from place to place in search of tenant farming jobs. The depression years pushed southerners, like the Joad family of eastern Oklahoma in John Steinbeck's *The Grapes of Wrath,* out on the road in search of opportunities in the West. Wartime labor shortages in the 1940s and work in automobile factories in the 1950s and 1960s attracted many southerners to Michigan. The Great Migration of African Americans to northern cities is only now being reversed as increasing numbers of African Americans (and whites) are returning to a more progressive and prosperous South and to familiar family communities.

During the years of the renaissance, a number of authors examined the relationship between the ideal of the farmer and "the myth of migration." Their characters migrate in search of the American dream—the stereotypical little white house with the white picket fence, the small plot of land, the chance for independence. In fact, these writers seem to reabsorb and embrace specifically American values in place of southern ones. This chapter deals specifically with novels concerned with migrations, journeys from one place to another, making the passage from one place to another in search of a better life that is grounded in the ideal of the farm. These novels are reminiscent of the stories of early settlement in the American South, and they suggest the American condition of the twentieth century. American agrarian life was increasingly influenced by the railroad, by the automobile, by the attraction of city life, by the destruction of big business farming practices. Americans found themselves repeating the pattern of their ancestors, but instead of following the trails of earlier wagon trains, they were taking to the hard road.

The American story of migration during the first half of the twentieth century seems to be very much a southern one. The journey captured the attention of southern writers, as southerners increasingly found themselves making the passage. Some, like Richard Wright in *Native Son* (1940) and *Black Boy* (1945), and Ralph Ellison in *Invisible Man* (1952), focused on the African American's journey from South to North in search of greater social, economic, and political equalities. By examining their own stories of migration, both Wright and Ellison point to the troublesome implications of racial prejudices in America at large. Also a novel about the southern journey northward, Harriette Arnow's *The Dollmaker* (1954) portrays a central character named Gertie Nevels who idealizes the agrarian life she leaves behind in rural Kentucky and who continues to struggle toward realization of her dream—a farm where she can raise her family. Although John Steinbeck is certainly not southern, he tells the story of southerners in search of the agrarian life in *The Grapes of Wrath* (1939). The Joads come from a family of farmers—not tenants—who are historically connected to the earth, and the novel is the epitome of the American story of movement in search of the ideal of the Jeffersonian small farm. Likewise, Elizabeth Madox Roberts's *The Time of Man* tells the story of Ellen Chesser and her family who are continually moving from farm to farm in search of work and to avoid troubles with the law. Their life is led on the road. Ellen continually desires a home of their own and land of their own, but that goal seems always out of their reach. In Willa Cather's *My Ántonia,* Jim Burden chases the ideal of agrarian life with Ántonia. From a family of immigrants, Ántonia is, at least within Burden's memory of her, able to live the ideal life of the settled American farmer. In contrast, Jim's adult life is spent in constant motion, traveling the railroad.

These stories of movement are specifically linked to the American ideals of the Jeffersonian farm, and although that ideal can be an elusive one, it frames the American experience and drives the American spirit. Although, as Eudora Welty once wrote, it is "the sense of place going with us still that is the ball of golden thread to carry us there and back and in every sense of the word to bring us home," southerners have increasingly found themselves on the road, once again part of the American journey, on a path necessary for survival.

In an introduction to the 2000 edition of *The Time of Man,* Wade Hall describes Ellen Chesser's life lived on the road as the traditional story of an individual's "journey to knowledge and selfhood" and as the "archetypal journey of the human family" (viii). The title of the book refers to the link human beings have with each other across the ages. "Your own short span on earth," explains Hall, is "your brief part of the long journey" of humanity (xv). Ellen, for example, thinks of the Native Americans who once peopled Kentucky, calling them "strange men," "a strange race doing things in strange ways" (87). Roberts writes that Ellen might not ever know why these earlier people chose certain pathways across the hills, but she is linked to them because of the action of movement, making the passage through human life. Roberts herself envisioned a novel that retold a story rooted in classical literature when she wrote in her journal that the "wandering tenant farmer" of the Upper South was "a symbol for an Odyssy [*sic*] of man as a wanderer, buffeted about by the fates and weathers" (xx). Calling the story "an ageless, placeless" one, Wade Hall describes the novel's style as "ceremonial" and "bardic" (xiv). As Ellen drives her cow down the road, following her family's wagon, it is as if they are "passing forward toward a moving destiny." Roberts describes them as moving en masse, "all moving down the turning roads and crossing lanes, going by some genius forward and on." They are continually moved on by a "forward-drawing force" (Hall xiv). Hall comments on the "rhythms of an ancient odyssey" (xiv) reflected in this passage and argues for a universal reading of Ellen's journey on the road.

Clearly, traveling the road leads Ellen to knowledge, growth, maturation, and womanhood. Without traveling, she will not make the passage into fulfillment. As a young woman, she lies in bed and can hear the sounds of horses galloping down the road as the "lonely horsehoofs" pound the frozen earth. Awakening to the sound, she feels at once "a thrill of pleasure, a joy at being awakened for any purpose, at feeling herself suddenly alive again" and then sorrow as the sound of the hoofbeats fades into the distance, leaving her behind in the darkness (112). As Ellen grows into womanhood, the road represents an opportunity for making friends, reaching sexual and emotional maturity, dating, and settling down with a husband and family. One of the defining relationships of Ellen's life is her girlhood friendship with a woman named Tessie who tells Ellen about her dreams of a proper home—one made of brick or stone, with a chimney covered in ivy. Tessie becomes a sort of mother figure for Ellen, as her own mother seems no longer able to dream of the prospects of a well-provisioned future. At one point, the young Ellen even leaves her parents' home to go in search of Tessie, who Ellen presumes is on the road with her husband and following work opportunities. Young men that she knows also travel the road in search of adventure like the young man of a song she hears, who leaves his beloved to go out into the world. As she hears "a beautiful tonk tonk tonk a-tonk of guitar strings out on the pasture road" (113) and J. B. Tarbell singing "Arkansas Traveler," she longs to know the world beyond her humble home. As a young woman, Ellen befriends other young people who live down the road, and they walk together to functions like church services and local gatherings. Ellen feels a sense of connectedness as they travel together. She feels herself as part of this group, "herself making part of the forms, herself merged richly with the design" (128–29). But the road also separates Ellen from the men she loves, including Jonas Prather, who goes in search of better work. She lives vicariously through him as she "expanded to take in the adventure and the new world and the new way between them" (194). Ultimately, though, Jonas's journey leads him to another woman, and Ellen is crushed by his decision to marry someone else.

Robert Penn Warren's 1963 essay entitled "Elizabeth Madox Roberts: A Life Within," reprinted in the 2000 edition of the novel, provides a framework for the novel, one focused in southern American history. Warren points to the stories of the frontier that Roberts heard as a child that linked her to earlier generations of her family that had helped to settle Kentucky. He explains, too, that "the imagination of the daughter Elizabeth was nourished on the long sweep of time from which the individual rises for his moment of effort and testing" (xviii). While the framework of a life's journey informs any reading of the book, this type of historical reading links Ellen's journey to American migration in search of an American dream. The Chessers and the married Ellen Kent and her family live lives of motion—not lives settled in a specific place.

While the road represents a journey through one's decisions and the consequences in life, Roberts shapes Ellen's journey as one headed toward the ideal of life on a farm that she works with her husband. Her journey is framed by a desire to work alongside a man, as she suggests when she thinks about Jonas: "All day her mind clung about his furrows or she hovered over his team and his plow in her thought, her hand on the plow handle or on the plow line, not merged with his but accompanying" (160). In another passage, she secretly spies on a farmhouse and farm family, hiding in the bushes and watching them as they prepare to leave their home for church. Ellen sees that the farmer's "land lay rolling in large plates, some of them green with high wheat, some faintly crisscrossed with corn rows, some in pasture." In an upper pasture she finds wild strawberries and a fence line of wild apple trees. When she comes to the house, she screens herself behind "tall weeds just beyond the vegetable garden." She questions, too, "if the farmer knew about the dull roof, now sharp in the sun, and if he knew how the yellow gables came out of the tree boughs, all set and still, fixed behind boughs, gables fitting into each other, snug and firm." Ellen has studied this world so closely that she figures she knows details about this farmer's home that he cannot see. The house is like many others she has seen as she and her family have gone "up and down roads," the "angles [of the houses] turning with the turning of roads" (18–19). Although Ellen may idealize the scene, a short quarrel between the farmer and his daughter points to the economic system that has left Ellen and her family traveling roads in search of work. The farmer insists that the young woman return to the house to lock the front door. "It pays not to take chances with people like that on the place," he says in reference to Ellen's family (19). Roberts notes the hypocrisy of the farmer when she writes that he and his family also carry their black Bibles in their hands as they head to church.

To Ellen, a piece of land to cultivate and a comfortable home represent security, but she always seems to be out of reach of that dream. Without ownership, that piece of land and that home can easily be taken from her family. When she thinks about a move to the Wakefield place, it is as if she "felt the feeling" of the Wakefield farm. She "felt"—and the key word here is "felt"—"what it would be to be a part of the land beyond the fence" (145). This is an experience that is at the core of her emotions and one that is rooted in her psyche. At the Bodine farm, Ellen looks at the farmhouse, "a yellow shape with points here and there, two red chimneys budding out of the roof," as it stands off in the distance among the tall trees. For Ellen, Roberts writes, the house "touched something she almost knew": "The treetops above the roof, the mist in the trees, the points of the roof, dull color, all belonging to the farmer, the yellow wall, the distance lying off across a rolling cornfield that was mottled with the wet and traced with lines of low corn—all these touched something settled and comforting in her mind, something like a drink of water after an hour of thirst, like a little bridge over a stream that ran out of a thicket, like cool steps going up into a shaded doorway" (14–15). The house represents something for which she hungers, something that will fulfill a deep and abiding longing.

Although the book is shaped around a rather long and complicated series of places that Ellen and her family move to, *The Time of Man* is about the desire for settlement. The book reflects the paradox that is central to American life. Out of necessity, and for survival, Ellen's family moves from place to place, yet it is the dream of property ownership and a better way of living on a settled piece of land that motivates them to continue to drive forward. When Jasper Kent tells his story, Ellen finds that it, like her father's, is "of labor, of wandering from farm to farm, of good seasons and bad, of good luck or evil" (277). Although Jasper leaves the community to look elsewhere for more profitable work, unlike Jonas, he returns home to marry Ellen. Ellen and Jasper often talk about their dreams of settling down on a farm to raise their family. His goal is to "find some fields worth a man's strength." He equates his manhood with physical power and endurance, and he farms with a vigor and passion. But eventually he says that he has become "plumb tired trafficken about, good land and bad as it comes" (284). He dreams, too, of "some pretty country where the fields lay out fair and smooth. A little clump of woodland. Just enough to shade the cows at noon" (285). Ellen tells Jasper of the future she envisions for them. That future is based in a domestic world but clearly rooted in an agrarian lifestyle: "our own house sometime, that belongs to us and all our own stock in the pastures. Three quick taps on the farm bell to call you to dinner. A rose to grow up over the chimney. A row of little flowers down to the gate" (305). Ellen's idyllic picture of life on the farm motivates and sustains her despite the desperate conditions under which she and her family live.

Ellen wishes to be rooted in a place by the tasks she must undertake as a farmer, but her aspirations also suggest the growing importance of a money economy in Kentucky. She dreams of a place where she can raise crops in a garden and care for her own poultry as a means of providing for her own family. But she also desires drawers, that is, pieces of furniture in her home and the things that can fill those drawers. Ellen hopes for visits from a peddler who will buy from her with the coins she so dearly loves to hear jingle in her pocket. Life in these hills does not seem solely attainable, then, through the crops of the earth.

Nevertheless, the earth is what has shaped Ellen's personality and her relationship with her husband. After Henry breaks his leg, when as he says, the earth "hit" him (253), Jasper arrives to help Ellen and her mother with the farming. "The conveyance of [Jasper's] arrival there had been the hoe"; he had come to them because of their need and because of his ability to work the earth (263). As Ellen works the fields in place of her father, the clods of earth seem at first to weigh her down. Ultimately, though, she finds that she can be the provider for her family. Her physical and spiritual beings gain strength from the soil as "the strength of her arms and her back and her thighs arose out of the soil" (263). Her very being melds into the landscape as her dreams of the future envelop "the fields, the silo, the barns, the spring, and the path" (313). Ellen becomes as tough and strong as the hard soil and rocks that she overturns to plant her crops.

Roberts's descriptions of farming families like the Chessers and the Kents characterize them as part of a larger mass, part of a larger movement of people down the roads. Ellen and her family are not alone. They are migrating Americans—much like the Joads in *The Grapes of Wrath*—who are described in terms ranging from "travelers" to "rovers" and "campers." "The people of the road" move along "all folded into one mass" (84), a sort of "pageant" as they move onward (30). Roberts suggests, however, that Henry Chesser's life is a good deal different from his father's. While Henry claims that he had "been all the way to Tennessee and then on to Georgia and back once and on to Tennessee once again" (14), he says that his father never left Luckett's Branch. Although the economic system has forced the Chessers to move from place to place in search of work, Henry suggests that he would have made the decision to keep moving. He is afraid he will "take root" somewhere, so he keeps to the road.

Passage along the road can leave a body worn and dispirited; the tolls can be steep, and the resting places can be uncertain. At the opening of the novel, as the Chessers make the passage from one farming job to another, from one temporary home to another, Ellen thinks of the physically painful and draining wagon rides she has taken along the roads. The "infected sores on her feet, great sores that would never quite heal and were always cut by the road dust" (30) might fade, but she will always carry their scars. When Ellen takes to the road to find Jonas, who has left the community for better farming opportunities elsewhere, she faces the dangers of the road by herself, walking in the direction Jonas has gone. She seems oblivious to the dangers of rape and theft, and she travels along in a sort of daze after she realizes that Jonas has abandoned her. The tolls of the road can thus be high. Roberts very specifically identifies the Chessers's house on the Orkey place as having been a tollhouse, with a stoop close to the roadside so that the toll taker was easily able to collect his monies. Travelers still often stop at the spring just across the road. Perhaps the highest toll that Ellen must pay in life is the death of her son Chick, who is born frail but whose delicate nature and playfulness bring joy to the Kent family. Born during a time of marital discord for Ellen and Jasper, Chick dies, leaving his parents closer because of the sorrow and anguish they share in experiencing both his short life and his passing.

Although Roberts comments in her novel about the continuing desire of the Chessers and the Kents to pursue the dream of a small farm, she also suggests that the economic values of the twentieth century have left the families homeless "people of the road." Ellen is sometimes cursed by property owners when she walks across their land. When landowner Scott MacMurtrie closes the road through his property, the men of the community are desperate to see that the road is reopened to allow them passage through. The road must be open for them to survive. When Jasper and Ellen move to the Goddard place, Jasper warns Ellen that she must stay up on the hill land they have been given to farm for themselves rather than ask for a small strip of land at the base of the hill or in the valley. "You stay up here on this here hill . . . where we belong now," he warns her. Jasper also becomes an earlier (and much more softened) version of Faulkner's Ab Snopes character when he is accused of burning farm property in two different communities and his family is forced to turn to the road in search of a place where Jasper can begin again with a cleared name. Although it is clear that Faulkner's Ab has burned barns,

Roberts leaves us to question whether or not Jonas committed the crimes. His volatile temper and his prison record suggest guilt, but a reader tends to have faith in his innocence because of the conditions of the tenant farming system that Roberts describes and because we wish his innocence for Ellen's sake. The road ultimately offers potential freedoms from a past that Roberts's characters struggle to leave behind.

Harriette Arnow's *The Dollmaker* presents an even more dramatic journey, one from southern Appalachia to Detroit, Michigan, as Gertie Nevels and her family join the masses of southerners who took part in the Great Migration to the industrialized North during World War II. During that era, southerners from depressed areas such as Appalachia found that their home communities no longer could sustain them, while the factories of the North and Midwest beckoned for workers to support the war effort and in the postwar years to build automobiles. Gertie makes the train journey with her children so that her family will survive. Her struggle to make the passage from agrarian Kentucky to industrial Detroit is heart-wrenching but ultimately necessary for the sake of her family.

The Kentucky scenes of *The Dollmaker* at first seem to suggest that an agrarian life is more desirable than life in the city. As the book opens, Gertie and her son Amos are making their way along the road to the nearest doctor when Gertie forces a car off the road, trying to obtain a ride to a medical facility. Although her only mode of transportation is a mule, Gertie is a physically empowering woman who is determined to save the life of her son. Early in the novel, we see her walking through a wooded Kentucky landscape, sure of her footing despite its being the middle of the night. Arnow also describes a bountiful meal that Gertie prepares for her family from the crops she has grown: "Gertie, sitting at the foot of the table with a lard bucket of sweet milk on one side of her, buttermilk on the other, a great platter of hot smoking cornbread in front, and other bowls and platters within easy reach, was kept busy filling glasses with milk, buttering bread, and dishing out the new hominy fried in lard and seasoned with sweet milk and black pepper. It was good with the shuck beans, baked sweet potatoes, cucumber pickles, and green tomato ketchup. Gertie served it up with pride, for everything, even the meal in the bread, was a product of her farming" (91). By the end of the novel, in Detroit, Gertie serves her family a meal that is sharply contrasted to the one described above because it is a product of industrialized, commercialized America: "spaghetti covered with a can of tomato soup, and smeared on top with a little dab of cheese" (595). The fruits of Gertie's labor in the earth suggest a purer and more wholesome way of living.

Despite this clear contrast between life in Kentucky and in Detroit, the death of her daughter Cassie, and Reuben's running away from home to return to Kentucky, scholars tend to read Gertie's move to Detroit as freeing and necessary. Arnow herself suggested such a reading when she explained in an interview, "Gertie, though it's hard to realize, felt more kindness to her from the people in the alley than she had ever known at home. She was always a stranger at home, especially with her mother" (Chung 3). Gertie must leave Kentucky in order to find her own voice. In Kentucky, she is controlled by her mother, a domineering woman who tells her that she must be in subjection to her husband and who preaches a fundamentalist-style religion as support for her gender views. Gertie even expresses regret that she is not able to be a stronger person in Kentucky: "She smelled it on herself, felt it on her oozy hands. She was a coward, worse than any of the others. If she could have stood up to her mother and God and Clovis and Old John, she'd have been in her own house this night" (148–49). Paradoxically, by following her husband to Detroit, Gertie sets aside her dream of a farm in Kentucky, but she also frees herself from the control of both her mother and her community.

Martha Billips Turner describes Gertie as "strangely out of keeping with those of the younger people around her and with her particular historical period" (3). Arnow, according to Turner, seems compelled to create a mid-twentieth-century character who represents Jefferson's ideal yeoman farmer in a "surprisingly pure form." Gertie works in Kentucky not for cash but for the products of the land. In working the land, she strives for "spiritual and moral compensation," not just economic independence. Calling her "agrarian and preindustrial," Turner argues that the chapters set in Kentucky actually question the feasibility of living the life of a self-sufficient farmer. For example, Gertie does not have enough money to buy shoes or glasses for her daughter Cassie, and although she has cut back on her family expenses for years, she only has the money to buy property after the death of her brother Henley. Even in Kentucky, she needs cash to survive and to raise her family with only the basic necessities. Kentucky may provide the bountiful meal that she raises and prepares for her family, but even Appalachia cannot remain immune to what Turner calls "the demands of a modern dollar economy" (2). Kentucky cannot provide Gertie and her family with the land she yearns for. "The modern world insists that its inhabitants—whether they live in rural Kentucky or industrial Detroit—earn money in some other, non-agricultural manner" (2).

Gertie must also leave Kentucky—or the "Southern garden"—in order to pursue her own destiny and to become a true artist, according to Elizabeth Harrison in her book *Female Pastoral: Women Writers Re-Visioning the American South*. Calling Gertie's autonomy "too aberrant" for her rural community, Harrison notes that owning a farm "would have cast her even more into the role of an iconoclast." Remaining in Kentucky would also have meant that Gertie's life was still constrained by the community's belief in "a God of retribution rather than mercy." Likewise, Harrison notes that Gertie would not have been able to be as self-sufficient after the end of World War II. For although war forces self-sufficiency on women, when war ends, society typically requires women to return to dependence on men (87–88). Harrison describes *The Dollmaker* as a *Künstlerroman* in which the artist must leave home in order to discover his or her identity as a true artist (94). At the end of the novel, Gertie's woodcarvings allow her family to survive, but they are not "art." Gertie destroys the "artifact"—her carving of Christ—in order to make the dolls she will sell to make money for her family to live. Harrison argues that by doing so, Gertie actually comes to value the creative process over the work of art itself. Pointing to Alice Walker's story "Everyday Use" and to Dee's appreciation of the monetary value of her mother's quilts rather than of the skill of crafting the quilts, Harrison explains that it is "the process of creation, not the end product, that counts most." While the art object is temporary, "it is the knowledge to create art—

to make more quilts or carve more figures in wood—that is essential." Although Gertie must temporarily put aside her identity as artist, she ultimately holds on to her ability to create art and to act as an independent person (97–98).

The Dollmaker is not only about Gertie's transition, about her migration outward from the South, but also about the collapsing boundaries between southern Appalachia and the rest of the world. Because of the products of industrialization rapidly becoming part of the everyday lives of Americans, people are moving more frequently across the boundary between the South and the world beyond. The landscape for the southerner is broader, but still confusing. Roberts describes a large world map that Mrs. Hull purchased by sending fifty cents to "somebody on the radio." It hangs on a nail that once held a roll of bologna in the Hull store. Now, people in the community study the map from across the meat counter, trying to identify the places where their men have gone to fight the war or to find work. The names of the places are strange, but they become increasingly familiar. Some of the women speak in soft voices that express their fear and awe of these places far away and "their own inability to imagine clearly the mountains, the oceans, the vast stretches of flat land, the time, and the weather that now lay between them and the man who only a little while ago had been no further away than across the table." Other of the women speak of the Aleutians, Paris, Okinawa, Louisville, London, Cincinnati, and Oak Ridge in the same way that they once spoke of a nearby hill or creek. In these times of trouble, their men working in factories or training at military camps do not seem as far away as those overseas. Places like England and France seem not so distant after the women look at the picture of India on the map (119–20).

As Gertie leaves for Detroit, the book embraces a decidedly American story of movement and transplantation. A southern story of a woman's desire for a farm where she can raise her family and her ability to express herself through her woodcarvings, farming, and childbearing evolves into a story that wrestles with the implications of an American migration. The novel comes to deal with the fact of motion—and indeed, the necessity of it—for the survival of both

Gertie's selfhood and for her family that finds itself entering a modern world that makes its way to even the backwoods of Kentucky. Movement is necessary for survival, and Gertie comes to recognize that the world is rapidly changing. As she leans over her gas stove in Detroit, frying some fish that she purchased not because she could identify it by name but because it was "cheap and unrationed," she thinks back to life in Kentucky with great nostalgia:

> The red ball of the winter's sun was going down behind the hills across the river. The cedar trees above the creek whispered among themselves in a rising night wind. The new milk was cooling on the porch shelf. Reuben was in the barn, the younger ones bringing in the wood and water, while Clytie fried fresh pork shoulder in the kitchen. On the stove hearth was a big pan of baked sweet potatoes, and pulled back on the stove where they wouldn't burn was a skillet of fresh-made hominy and another of late turnip greens. It had been a good fall for the turnips she had planted. She was cutting up the soap she'd made that day from the guts of her big fattened hog. Every once in a while she'd step off the porch and look a little south, but mostly west; that would be above her father's house, where the new moon showed first. (265)

Indeed, though, the sun is setting. For Gertie, the ideal at the end of the Nevels' struggle to survive will always revolve around the ideal of the farm, whether or not they remain in Detroit. Her dream will always be of a small farm where she can be self-sufficient and nurture her children. But that will be the ideal. Nevertheless, the book comes to focus not on the goal but on the journey made.

One of my students who gave a class report on John Steinbeck's *The Grapes of Wrath* described the novel as a book about marching. It is a very apt description for explaining both the significance of the book's title and the movement of the novel. Marching, too, suggests the endurance of characters like Gertie Nevels and Ellen Chesser. As the Joads of eastern Oklahoma make their way westward along Route 66 into California in search of the fruits of the earth, they—like Gertie—leave behind a land their ancestors wrestled from the Indians and farmed in the tradition of Jefferson's yeoman farmer. It is the desire to find a better life on better soil that leads the Joads to

California, in search of an American dream. As northern soldiers once marched to Julia Ward Howe's "Battle Hymn of the Republic," symbolically taking up the sword for God whose "truth is marching on," the Joads' march is one that perpetuates an American mission to reach the promised land of California, to journey westward in search of better opportunities that are intimately tied with an American ideal.

Willa Cather seems to idealize the small farm and Ántonia's life with her family in rural Nebraska, but Joseph Urgo argues that most readers of Cather's *My Ántonia* would probably choose to live Jim Burden's life rather than Ántonia Cuzak's. Jim's established life in the city is closer to what most of us strive for, even though we might greatly value Ántonia's home-building and nurturing of her family, her family's ability to raise their own food, and her garden that recalls a long-lost Eden. Urgo explains that Jim, "essentially a migratory American," focuses in his story on the crossing of Ántonia and other European immigrants because he has come to recognize that their passage is actually "the archetype of his own restlessness" (55). Jim Burden's life story is one of a succession of places. Even though at novel's end he may say that he felt as if he were home again when he visits Ántonia's family, he has no intention of settling in to Nebraska farm life. Urgo writes that Cather defines "home" as "the places we leave." (Or, he qualifies, "if it is not, home is the place to which we have reluctantly returned or in which we have got ourselves stuck.") But for Cather, he maintains, "home is understood relative to spatial movement" (56).

The experience of making the crossing is actually what "fires Burden's imagination and ambition for a lifetime" (60), according to Urgo. Living in New York and working as legal counsel for one of the great western railways, Jim Burden has done what Ántonia's father, Mr. Shimerda, could not do. He has traveled west without regrets for making the journey. Mr. Shimerda is buried at the crossroads because he is unable to embrace his new country and leave behind his homeland in Eastern Europe. Homesickness leads him to suicide. "To survive in Cather's American context is to possess the mutable skills of the traveler and to keep a clear distinction between the ideas that fire the imagination and the physical manifestation of those concepts,"

Urgo argues. Jim can carry his image of Ántonia with him through his life. As Urgo explains in some detail, we carry images around with us so that we can make it through our daily lives, although the images that we value and that shape us may directly contradict the lives we actually live. Jim, for example, may carry the image of Nebraska farm life with him as an ideal, even though he lives in constant motion, traveling the railways for his job in the city. Jim's professional success lies in the fact that he values his roots in rural Nebraska, the famed plow set against the midwestern sunset, and his relationship with Ántonia. "In Cather's vision," Urgo writes, "the images we carry, the images that define our sense of moral values and self-worth, often directly and quite productively contradict what we are and what we do" (71–72).

Jim Burden thus shares with Ellen Chesser, Gertie Nevels, and the best known of the depression-era travelers, the Joads, a story of migration. All southern-born, they become distinctly American in making the passage. As the Virginia-born Jim considers his Ántonia at the end of Cather's novel, he writes that if he closes his eyes, he can still hear the rumbling sound of the wagon wheels on the road as he and Ántonia made their way to their new Nebraska homes. That road, he concludes, is the one that brings them together once again. As Ellen and her family load up their wagon at the end of *The Time of Man,* Roberts notes that they will load as much on their wagon as they can carry with them, but the rest they must leave behind. As their wagon moves along, "they asked no questions of the way but took their own turnings" (395). The ideal that frames their values and dreams is the image of the American farmer working the earth as a self-sufficient, independent soul. The image of the farming Cuzaks on their Nebraskan farm "fire[s] the imagination" of Jim Burden, and likewise the image of a comfortable home on a self-sustaining farm is what drives Ellen Chesser and Gertie Nevels to seek sufficient, comfortable living conditions for their families. Both Ellen and Gertie earn their independence providing for their families by working a farm. Both women journey toward a similar ideal—one based in the Jeffersonian tradition of the yeoman farmer—that allows them to deal with the trials of everyday life. Willa Cather sets up the "heroic" plow on an upland farm in *My Ántonia* so that it stands against the sun, with its disk, handles, tongue, and share, "black against the molten red." Although this "picture writing on the sun" celebrates a life that is fast disappearing (183), the image carries Jim through his life. The search—the migration—is what defines Jim as an American. So, too, are Gertie and Ellen and the Joads on an American journey—no longer just a southern one. Their goals of the American farm may be elusive, but it is the passage from one place to another that now defines them.

While making the passage can be difficult enough, the migrant must also lighten the load if the journey is to be a successful one. In other words, the past must often be left behind. Ma Joad clearly understands this as she sorts through the items she has placed in a stationary box she had hidden in their Oklahoma home. Removing only the items that might later be sold to support her family, she places the box containing letters, photographs, and newspaper clippings on the fire. Grandpa and Grandma both die as the family makes the passage westward, showing that the living past cannot be taken with the Joads. The land in Oklahoma that has sustained their family for generations now blows away with the Dust Bowl winds, forcing the Joads to remake themselves by journeying to California. Ellen realizes the clear necessity of moving on and not looking back at the end of *The Time of Man*. Once again accused of burning another farmer's property, Jasper is forced to leave their tenant house in search of a new home for his family. Uncertain as to where they will go, the family quickly loads their property onto their wagon and hurries down the road, "without waiting to dispute of ways or to talk of destinations" (393). Ellen remains solid in her faith that they will find "some better country. Our own place maybe. Our trees in the orchard. Our own land sometime. Our place to keep . . . " (394). Ellen and her family are continually trying to leave the past behind, but for them, there is always the fear that the past will follow them, that they will not be able to begin anew.

The focus in these novels is not the traditional story of the southern attachment to place but the journey the characters take as they evolve within new communities. By the end of *The Grapes of Wrath*, the Joads have begun to define themselves not by the pejorative term

"Okie" but instead as part of the larger human community. In Weed-patch and in the actions of Jim Casy, Tom Joad comes to recognize the necessity of working for the betterment of the lives of the mi-grant workers who face poverty and disillusionment because of the Great Depression. Steinbeck's inter-chapters also emphasize the in-terconnectedness of the families that made the journey west and the similar burdens they carry. Likewise, as *The Time of Man* closes, Ellen Chesser recognizes that she is part of a collective memory related to her gender. She sees herself as merging with Nellie, her mother, in "the long memory she had of her . . . through the numberless places she had lived or stayed and the pain she had known." Ellen sees her own life merging with her mother's, hardly able to separate one from the other, "both flowing continuously and mounting" (381).

When Robert Penn Warren wrote that "history is the big myth we live, and in our living, constantly remake," he suggested that hu-man beings revise both our personal and our communal histories. We do so as a way to cope with the present, as an effort to maintain or perpetuate our own political or religious opinions, as a means to make changes in our lives more palatable. The South has always been a region of the mind, although we may attempt to lay claim to its boundaries on a physical map. Yet as the physical boundaries of the areas of the United States that labeled themselves as southern be-came increasingly blurred in the first half of the twentieth century, writers such as Roberts, Arnow, Cather, and Steinbeck recognized that the southern region of the mind needed to lay claim to a broader identity that framed southerners within the context of American so-ciety as a whole. That broader identity lays claim not to the plantation myths of the Old South but to a new South tightly bound to American democratic ideals.

In many ways, too, the lives of a large number of the best-known writers of the Southern Renaissance reflect the American drive to mi-grate. Robert Penn Warren, Katherine Anne Porter, Zora Neale Hurs-ton, Jean Toomer, Harriette Arnow, John Crowe Ransom, Allen Tate, and Thomas Wolfe (and, of course, many others) led lives of migration and movement. Their unsettled lives took them beyond their home places. Educational and job opportunities, adventure, research, escape

—the reasons often came down to matters related to their work as writers. Some might believe that many of our best southern writers became writers *because* they left the South. In a similar fashion, Cather's Jim Burden cannot be the artist who tells his story until he leaves rural America. Gertie Nevels does not recognize the true value of her ability to create until she moves to Detroit and discovers that she must sell her art to provide for her family. All follow what Eudora Welty called "the golden thread . . . to bring us home." But even for Welty, who studied outside the South as a young woman, that journey home could only be made after she left home for the world beyond.

Conclusion

A LEGACY FOR THE SOUTH

In the years of the first Southern Literary Renaissance, especially during the 1920s and 1930s, southern writers became increasingly interested in dealing not only with the failure and defeat of the Lost Cause and the plantation South but also with the lives of everyday southerners and the potential for healing and renewal. In large part this shift came about because of an interest in redefining southern history within the context of Jeffersonian agrarianism and democracy rather than emphasizing plantation culture. The twentieth century was clearly the age of the common man and woman in American literature, and for southern literature. The mythologies connected to Jeffersonian democracy and agrarianism also shaped new mythologies for the South that gave new power and new hope to a culture trapped in a myth of failure and loss. Many writers of the modern South embraced the agrarian model of the farmer to suggest that a new mythology for the South was possible and also necessary. Not only writers such as the Nashville Agrarians, Ellen Glasgow, and Jesse Stuart but also many others who followed the first Southern Literary Renaissance recognized the significance of the plain people within the framework of southern history and culture.

This web entangles writers like Eudora Welty, who wrote stories of healing and renewal that point to the value of living in rural communities close to the soil. In her 1946 novel *Delta Wedding*, for example, Welty makes use of a theme of reconciliation, a popular concept in the nineteenth-century South, but she reframes that idea within the context of the needs and the possibilities of life in the twentieth century. During the antebellum and postbellum periods, for instance, stories of marriage by southern writers suggested the importance of reunion between North and South but often portrayed the southern marriage partner as persuading the Yankee over to southern ways. Concerned over the growing rift between North and South, Caroline Hentz, for example, published *The Planter's Northern Bride* in 1854. Stories of marriage between southerners and northerners became particularly numerous in the years following the war as stories of reconciliation. Thomas Nelson Page's *Red Rock: A Chronicle of Reconstruction* (1898), Joel Chandler Harris's 1898 short story "A Comedy of War," and John Fox, Jr.'s *The Little Shepherd of Kingdom Come* (1903) are perhaps some of the best-known examples.

What is particularly interesting about *Delta Wedding* is that reconciliation is not between North and South but between the farming and plantation Souths. The marriage of Troy Flavin to Dabney Fairchild first holds uncertainty that the match is a good one because Dabney is "marrying down." From the far-away Tishomingo, Troy is the Fairchild family's overseer on their Delta plantation. When one of the Fairchild children, Little Battle, playfully pretends to be the bridegroom, he says, using a voice like Troy's, that he is from "up near the Tennessee line. Mighty good people up there. Have good sweet water up there, everlasting wells" (242). Little Battle continues to poke fun by explaining that as Troy he is not lonesome up in the hills because with his sister's marriage to a supervisor, "Now we enjoy a mail and ice route going by two miles from the porch" (243).

Although the scene suggests the typical dynamics between a young boy and his engaged teenage sister, Little Battle's words also point to the superior attitude of the Delta Fairchilds that they generally keep masked. Nevertheless, the union represents the coming together of Delta plantation culture and upland farming culture, and Welty implies that the Fairchild family will be strengthened by this union. When quilts arrive from Troy's mother in the foothills, with wedding blessings for "manly sons, loving daughters," Welty suggests the Fairchild family line will be continued with vitality and promise

(149). After the wedding, Troy plans to continue overseeing the Fairchild property, and Troy and Dabney are to settle at Marmion, to finish the house so that it will be a true home of the Fairchild clan.

In reaction to the heroic qualities of a character like Troy, however, Flannery O'Connor suggests that the mythology of the common man and woman cannot fulfill the potential of a Christ-based life. While Welty's story of reconciliation mends the South, O'Connor wants to break down the model of the independent, self-sustaining farmer. Believing that a return to agrarian living was impossible in the modern world, O'Connor wrote in her last year of life to "A," "It's futile of course like 'woodman, spare that tree'" (*Habit* 566). Frequently making use of stories of courtship, O'Connor breaks down the myth to make a point that figures prominently in her theology. A much anthologized and much studied group of stories by O'Connor provides a particularly strong example. Called O'Connor's "farm stories," the group includes "Good Country People," "The Life You Save May Be Your Own," "Revelation," "Greenleaf," and "A Circle in the Fire." The stories all tell of women (often mothers and daughters) who live on and work farm property. Despite what might first appear to be stories of a promising independence and self-sufficiency for women, O'Connor, in her typical interest in leaving her characters and her readers open to the possibility of new faith in God and Christ, forces us to recognize the folly of such living. These women characters may exemplify the essential values and goals of democratic agrarian living in owning their property and being essentially free from outside, male control and able to make their own decisions. Nevertheless, characters like Hulga in "Good Country People" and the mother in "The Life You Save May Be Your Own" cannot see beyond themselves to a higher significance. Because they have turned inward, O'Connor wants to open them to other possibilities, in particular, an awareness that ultimate truths must be found in a higher power.

With characteristic concern for names and naming, O'Connor frames "Good Country People" with a title that points to the inconsistencies of Mrs. Hopewell's nature. She "hopes well" of people, believing that the Freemans who work for her are not "trash" but "good country people." Mrs. Hopewell believes she can look beyond Mrs.

Freeman's annoyances that lost her husband his last job: "She realized that nothing is perfect and that in the Freemans she had good country people and that if, in this day and age, you get good country people, you had better hang onto them" (272–73). She believes, too, that the Bible salesman Manley Pointer is "good country people" and continues to believe so at the end of the story. As Mrs. Hopewell and Mrs. Freeman dig for the "evil-smelling onion shoot" (291), Mrs. Hopewell continues to recognize Manley as "simple," "good country people." He has violated Mrs. Hopewell's daughter, but Mrs. Hopewell will never understand.

Increasingly, southern writers in the years since the first Southern Literary Renaissance have been dealing with the opportunities for and the necessities of stories of survival. Madison Smartt Bell takes a national perspective that emphasizes the importance of racial healing and of healing not only the southern land, but also the earth's soil in order to safeguard the future of humanity. In Bell's *Soldier's Joy* (1989), for example, Thomas Laidlaw returns home after the Vietnam War to wander the woods on his family farm and to play his banjo. Laidlaw returns to a home that is showing the wear of years and of inattention: "Behind the house cleared ground rose and leveled out at a small dug pond with a barn beginning to fall down beside it, and then climbed more steeply to the tree line. The hill pasture was raked with fresh red gullies and the garden on the low side of the house had gone to weeds for two years and most of the rooms of the house itself were full of the plunder of white-trash tenants and God only knew what went on in the woods, but Laidlaw didn't care" (3).

He has been crippled both physically and emotionally by war, but in relearning the fingering for a song called "Cripple Creek," Laidlaw regains some faith in his own abilities and recaptures a link to his own past (14). At first he is afraid to look at his own hand or to move his feet, but as the "fireflies [signal] phosphorescent *green green green* from the dark outside," Laidlaw's hand falls "into the beat as simply as he'd had faith it one day would, as if it had emerged from some amnesiac stupor to recall what it had really always known how to do." Laidlaw does not, however, remain isolated in his own music but ultimately joins a bluegrass band and thereby symbolically returns to the human community he has avoided the first half of the novel.

Bell's novel is principally concerned with healing—healing the southern earth and the relationships between blacks and whites. Initially, as Laidlaw reenters his community, he also feels the weight of racial prejudice. Bell says that in the novel he wanted to show "how much testing [a friendship between a black man and a white man] could take in the South, in that kind of community" ("Booklist" 1469). Laidlaw was raised on the same farm in Middle Tennessee as Rodney Redmon, an African American who also served in Vietnam. Laidlaw's father owned the land and Redmon's father worked it. Although Laidlaw and Redmon eventually form a strong friendship, they must first overcome feelings of jealousy and guilt. Because Laidlaw's father did not give him the attention he deserved, he found a father figure in Rodney's father. Understandably, Rodney finds himself dealing with his own jealousy about his father's relationship with Laidlaw. Laidlaw and Redmon's relationship is a very complex one. As *Soldier's Joy* comes to a close, Laidlaw offers to give Redmon prime land on the farm so that the two of them might live in separate houses on the property and farm the land together.

A more national history also haunts the two men as they fight against the Klan in a battle reminiscent of their days in Vietnam in the last scene of the novel. At times, Laidlaw seems to forget that he is in Tennessee fighting the Klan—not in Vietnam. After a machine gun makes "a thudding blur across his chest" (463), Laidlaw lies bleeding in the bed of a pickup truck that is taking him to safety. At first, even Redmon's words, "I won't let you go," seem of little help (465). Yet Redmon is determined that Laidlaw survive. "Don't you quit on me now . . . Hey, we still got a house to build," he tells Laidlaw (464–65). The reader does not know at the end of the novel if Laidlaw lives or dies. Ultimately, though, what is most important is that Laidlaw attempts to heal racial wounds and struggles for a cause, trying to bring change to his South. Through the southern earth, by settling together on the farm and building houses, Redmon believes his relationship with Laidlaw and their individual ties to the southern earth can be mended.

Laidlaw does survive in another of Bell's novels, *Save Me, Joe Louis*, another book about a southerner who needs "saving" and who finds some promise for that salvation in his Tennessee home place. Actually, Laidlaw lives down the road from Macrae's elderly, blind father. But Macrae, along with Charlie, his accomplice in crime and a fellow southerner, does not return to Tennessee for an intentional rediscovery of his roots; instead, the AWOL Macrae flees there to escape the law. In New York City, Macrae and his partner Charlie force their victims to withdraw money from cash machines. Macrae is a sort of gentleman bandit, "a professional mugger who's always very polite and listens patiently to his victims" ("Booklist" 1469).

Nothing looks familiar to Macrae, "down home" now in Tennessee. "Rows of jerry-built houses," a new "flat square high school building," and "black, oily, brand-new" parking lots confuse him (220–21). Ultimately, however, by returning to Tennessee, and thus to an old girlfriend named Lacy, Macrae seems to find stability and comfort from what the book's jacket calls the "topsy turvy world of perpetual distemper." By the end of the novel, Macrae and Lacy look at each other "as if they [are] seeing each other for the first time in their lives" (351). In some very distinct ways, then, Macrae is akin to Thomas Laidlaw. *Soldier's Joy* and *Save Me, Joe Louis* are clearly shaped by a pattern of escape and return. Both Macrae and Laidlaw escape into worlds beyond the South into patterns of life far removed from their rural upbringings, yet in returning home, they find the possibilities of healing and closure.

Macrae's potential renewal is also strongly influenced by Laidlaw. Laidlaw recognizes what Macrae is, and he has an insight into the problems that Macrae faces. Laidlaw even encourages Macrae to play the songs that he had taught him as a teenager, when the sound of music drew Macrae to Laidlaw's place, up "through the fields" (239). But Macrae's "fingertips [are] tender, so long it [has] been since he played" (238). They try singing a song called "Soldier's Joy," a clear reference to Bell's novel of renewal and recovery. But for Macrae, although this return South holds potential for him as more than escape from the law, in the end, Macrae is once again drawn into crime, as he, Charlie, and Porter hold up a Wells Fargo truck. Their attempt is botched when Charlie kills the two guards. The three men flee Tennessee for the Carolina coast. Ultimately, though, Macrae returns home to Tennessee to bury his dead father, to reunite with Lacy, and, in self-defense, to kill the pursuing Charlie. Now, only Macrae and Lacy know the crime that he has committed; they share the secret of Macrae's involvement in the robbery and in Charlie's death. At the end of the novel, Macrae believes he can begin anew on the farm with Lacy.

Other writers of the contemporary South such as Wendell Berry suggest the importance of looking at the environment from a global perspective and recognizing the dangers of ignoring this approach. Berry is a particularly good example because he has chosen to live the life of the rural farmer in Kentucky. In "The Work of Local Culture," an essay that provides a contemporary approach to the Agrarian argument, Berry writes of human communities in general, suggesting that a human community "must collect leaves and stories, and turn them to account. It must build soil, and build that memory of itself—in lore and story and song—that will be its culture" (154). According to Berry, in order to exist, human communities must be in the business of both "holding local soil and local memory in place" by exerting "a sort of centripetal force." Yet, Berry says, our contemporary society generates a centripetal force that is centered not in the local, but in our industrialized cities. Thus the centrifugal force that operates against that centripetal force "returns to the countryside not the residue of the land's growth to refertilize the fields, not the learning and experience of the greater world ready to go to work locally." Instead, the greater world sends back to the countryside manufactured goods, pollution, and garbage (155). This view of the conflict between the southern countryside and the city seems implicit in Madison Smartt Bell's *Save Me, Joe Louis*. Macrae's salvation from crime rests in living with Lacy on his isolated farm, far from the violence of life in the northern city.

In his 1977 book entitled *The Unsettling of America,* Berry emphasizes the importance of as many Americans as possible sharing in land ownership. Through this bond, people create not only an economic relationship to the land, but also an "investment of love and work, by family loyalty, by memory and tradition." "The old idea is still full of promise," he says, for that old idea is "potent with healing and with health." Through land ownership, the individual has the ability to turn away from the "big-time promising and planning" of the government "to confront in himself, in the immediacy of his own circumstances and whereabouts, the question of what methods and ways are best." In effect, land ownership, according to Berry, "proposes the independent, free-standing citizenry that Jefferson thought to be the surest safeguard of democratic liberty" (45).

When Berry wrote his preface to the second edition of *The Unsettling of America* (1986), those problems he saw in 1977 had only intensified. The central questions of his introduction seem particularly important ones for considering the future of America and of humanity as a whole: "Are we, or are we not, going to take proper care of our land, our country? And do we, or do we not, believe in a democratic distribution of usable property?" Berry says that the responses to these questions are currently negative ones. Soil erosion rates, he explains, are now worse than they were during the years of the Dust Bowl. Water is being overused and wasted, and toxic chemicals are polluting our land and becoming an increasingly serious problem. "We are closer every day to the final destruction of private ownership not only of small family farms, but of small usable properties of all kinds" (viii). He continues, though, to point to the healing powers of land ownership and to warn, too, that in losing our connection to the land, we also lose our individual freedoms that were won by the founders of our country.

Berry, as well as other southern writers, may continue to embrace these democratic themes and ideals as a means of asserting their arguments for the survival of the South, but perhaps just as importantly, southern literature has itself become a much more democratic literature within the last several decades. Fred Hobson points out in his essay included in *The Future of Southern Letters* that southern history has been a history of exclusion and in past years so has the region's literature and even the scholarship about that literature (81). Hobson, though, suggests a much more hopeful present and future for southern literature when he points out that in the last twenty-five years, there has been a "wave in the democratizing" of southern literature (74). Like American literature, in general, southern literature has also been expanding its boundaries, although perhaps at a slower rate than literatures from other parts of the country, according to Hobson (73–74).

Because southern literature is now much more democratic, there is understandably more diversity in the region's storytellers. More people—and different types of people—are able to tell their stories. In an essay included in *The History of Southern Women's Literature*, Linda Tate explains that contemporary literature by southern women is "very much a postsegregation literature." No longer do southern women writers dwell on the "apology and the purging of guilt" that played a prominent role in modern southern writing. Instead, the interest is on "the reclaiming of one's voice, one's own citizenship in the South" (491). According to Tate, women writers of the contemporary South are interested in "healing the pain of the past so that they and their characters may live more freely and joyously in the present." A particularly meaningful comparison, according to Tate, suggests the differences between modern and contemporary southern literature. "Quentin Compson has met his match in Alice Walker's Celie," says Tate. Celie, "transformed as she is from brutalized oppression to joyful love, stands as an emblem of the new era" (492).

Indeed, Walker specifically uses imagery connected with planting, with the lives of women living in rural areas, to suggest the value and the promise of woman's creativity in her essay entitled "In Search of Our Mother's Gardens." In the same way that the facts of Walker's mother's life are set in the rural landscape of Georgia, so, too, is Walker's art rooted there. As Connie Schomburg explains in "Southern Women Writers in a Changing Landscape," gardens for Walker "represent an individual's attempt to bring order to chaos" and "serve as a statement not only about the resilience of southern black women, but about their often overlooked but nonetheless magnificent artistry" (483). We may not know the names of these women who down through the generations passed on a "creative spark, the seed of the flower they themselves never hoped to see." Their seed is planted like Janie's in *Their Eyes Were Watching God*, so that women like Walker can now tell their stories. These generations of women may not have been able to read "plainly" what Walker describes as a "sealed letter" (240), but they "save[d] de text" for other women, and it was through their art that they created in a rural domestic world—a world where they farmed and cooked their produce and sewed—that the text was saved. Walker points to her own mother and to the beautiful flowers of her garden. In "her face, as she prepares the Art that is her gift, is a legacy of respect she leaves to me, for all that illuminates and cherishes life." Walker's mother passed down to her daughter a "respect for the possibilities—and the will to grasp them" (241–42).

In effect, Walker's search for "our mothers' gardens" is essential to the transformation of a character like Celie in *The Color Purple* and the place Linda Tate conceives for her as "emblem of the new era." To go "in search of our mothers' gardens" means specifically for most southern writers a journey into the rural, agricultural past of the South. Walker's search for Zora Neale Hurston's grave has become an engrained part of the history of southern women's writing. In effect, Walker's search for that unmarked grave in a Florida cemetery also suggests that Hurston's story of Janie and the seeds she is able to plant at the end of *Their Eyes Were Watching God* found fertile ground in the contemporary South for writers like Alice Walker. Walker writes in her essay "In Search of Our Mothers' Gardens" about her mother, who worked tirelessly to care for her family by sewing clothing, towels, and even the sheets on their beds. She worked hard throughout the summer canning fruits and vegetables, and in the winter she made the quilts that the family used to keep warm at night. The day began before sunup for her and ended late at night. She worked alongside her husband in the fields—"not behind," Walker notes. The gardens of Walker's title are the gardens of inspiration, of creativity. They are the gardens—the art—that are created by woman, whether it be a woman's creations in the kitchen, in the sewing room, or on the printed page. But Walker goes in search of the lives and gardens of women who were not famous, as she says, who lived lives typical of the larger mass of people.

At the heart of Walker's search is her desire to find the "secret of what has fed that muzzled and often mutilated, but vibrant, creative spirit that the black woman has inherited." That "creative spirit pops out in wild and unlikely places to this day," even though the history of African American women might suggest that the hardships they have lived through are ones that are far from conducive to lives of creativity and art. When can a woman like Walker's mother, who worked day and night to care for her family, find the time "to know or care about freeing the creative spirit?" (238–39). Suggesting that creativity and art only seem to be valued when they are connected to traditional arts such as poetry and fiction writing, the visual arts such as painting and sculpting, Walker points out that we overlook the importance of other sorts of art that have been the creative work of women for generations, creative work that is tied specifically to the earth and to rural lives.

In a similar fashion, the rural landscape—specifically the peach orchard—of Dori Sander's 1990 novel *Clover* seems to have healing powers not only for the young girl Clover, who is the first-person narrator of the novel, but also for the division between blacks and whites in the South. Described in *The Literature of the American South* as "a model for black writers embracing the South," author Dori Sanders writes from her own family's experience raising peaches and selling them from a roadside market. "The land and its produce," according to the editors of *The Literature of the American South,* are "central to that reconciliation." Although they certainly do not claim that the South is free of racism and violence associated with racism, the editors of the book suggest that African American writers of the contemporary South are "nonetheless in a generation that has reclaimed that soil in an effort to make it sprout healthy black lives." African American writers of today, they argue, "claim the soil as their own, claim their right to American democracy and southern heritage in a conscious reintegration process that was not apparent four decades ago" (589).

Over the course of the novel, Clover is physically and spiritually healed. A ten-year-old black girl who lost her father within hours of his marriage to a white woman, Clover finds herself living with a woman she does not know, someone she believes she should push away because of her race. Clover's mother and her caregiver grandfather are both dead, and so now is her father, who was killed in a car accident by a drunk driver. When Sara Kate, Clover's stepmother, decides to remain in Round Hill to raise Clover, it is as if, Clover says, there are two people living in their house—"Together, yet apart." Their house is quiet, except for the music that Sara Kate sometimes plays, and they "move about in separate ways." "We," Clover says, are "like peaches. Peaches picked from the same tree, but put in separate baskets" (100). Both Clover and Sara Kate need healing. There is, on the one hand, the obvious reference to the loss they both feel with the death of Gaten—one for a husband and the other for a father. But Clover also suffers physically from a pulled muscle and an eye injury, and she tries to hide her physical ailments from Sara Kate because, as she says, she does not want to be dragged off to the doctor's office. In large part, however, Clover is more concerned with refusing to share her personal feelings, her pain, with anyone else.

The peach orchard also plays a central role in the evolution of that relationship. Although Gaten was a school principal, Clover says that her father would not spend much money on school clothes because his money was tied up in the peach crop. Farming, he explained to her, is "a card game . . . The weather can call its hand anytime. And in a second, the game is over" (119–20). But Clover also remembers that for "some school paper," her father wrote about the way in which the natural world links farmers together: "Between farmers, there is that communality of souls. In their own special way, farmers have a unique form of religion. All are at times forced to share common experiences and hardships. Together, with usually the same reverence and respect, they bow to the weather for the outcome of their crops" (139). As the relationship between Clover and Sara Kate first evolves, they seem to have little to share—and little brings them together except for their grief over Gaten. They are not that "communality of souls." Sara Kate stays in the house, in the air conditioning, working on her drawings that she sells to textile makers and wallpaper producers. Clover's Aunt Everleen works in the heat, picking peaches and selling them at the fruit stand, taking care of the family business while Sara Kate stays away from it, perhaps not yet feeling a part of the family and of the peach orchard that is at the focal point of their communal life.

Sara Kate tries to connect with Clover and to become a part of the family through attempts specifically tied to the peach orchard. She mentions that she loves peaches, and she expresses this opinion of peaches with such intensity that Clover finally tells her, "You know something, Sara Kate, it wouldn't hurt you one bit to come up to that peach shed for some peaches." Sara Kate seems to have wanted this invitation all along. Her eyes light up and she thanks Clover for inviting her, but all Clover can think is "Imagine that. Thanking somebody for something that's part theirs in the first place!" (130–31). Clover mentions the homemade peach jelly and the fresh peach cobbler that they eat at their house, but Sara Kate only eats the jelly in small spoonfuls from the jar. She does not dig deep into the jar; instead, she eats the jelly sparingly, as if it is a great treat to her but something she cannot share fully. Clover explains in her narration that she has heard people who live together start to look alike. Even though they have been living together for some time, Clover believes she and Sara Kate will never look like each other, though they are beginning to act like each other. Nevertheless, by the end of the novel, Clover explains that although she thought she stood out because of the color of her skin at a cookout she attended with Sara Kate and her white suitor, she now concludes, "Come to think of it, maybe I didn't stand out so much after all." As a child is a product of what she learns about racial prejudices from the people around her, Clover now seems willing to look beyond race. She explains that after Sara Kate has spent time in the sun for a couple of weeks, she is dark enough that she can "almost pass for one of us." Clover concludes, "I guess it's the way she wanted to look" (174).

Ultimately, though, the family is brought together because of a life-and-death situation that occurs at the peach orchard. When Gaten's brother, Jim Ed, is stung by yellow jackets at the end of the novel, Sara Kate tells Everleen to run for help while she and Clover fight to get the yellow jackets off and to resuscitate Jim Ed. Jim Ed is highly allergic to bee stings, and Sara Kate knows it. She fights through the yellow jackets and saves Jim Ed's life. We learn, too, that a thoughtless customer dumped a basket of peaches after discovering a nearby tree with larger fruit. The basket was dumped beside some yellow jacket nests, and Jim Ed was unlucky enough to fall off the tree into the peaches and the swarming insects. As he recuperates, Sara Kate learns to drive a tractor and takes up responsibilities with the peaches. By the end of the novel, the family and people from the community gather at Clover and Sara Kate's house after the peach shed closes at night: "After the yellow jacket thing, they walk over almost every evening after we close the peach shed. They sit out under the big oaks in the front yard and talk until dark. Gaten's hammock is still stretched between two of the trees. Sometimes Jim Ed will rest there until it's time to go home. It's almost like old times" (183). As farmers tied together by their crop, the family finds reconciliation.

In a similar fashion, southern writers like Bobbie Ann Mason also seek a return to the South—a return to agrarian roots. After writing throughout her career about the southerner's displacement from a rural landscape, Mason seems to have sought reconciliation with her agrarian roots in Kentucky after years of being away from the state. Although the possibilities for young women beyond the borders of Kentucky and Mason's own desire to leave the rural western Kentucky of her roots were such that she moved to New York City after her graduation from the University of Kentucky, she returned in the early 1990s to live in the Lexington area on a farm.

Such possibilities of a return seem not always to have been offered, at least from Mason's perspective. Connie Schomburg explains in "Southern Women Writers in a Changing Landscape" that Mason tends to portray her contemporary women characters as disconnected from the land, while her women characters living earlier in the twentieth century are "involved with and strongly identified with the land." "Like Mason herself," Schomburg argues, "these contemporary characters may express an appreciation for the old ways, but are for the most part uninterested in 'maintaining the Garden'" (483). Correspondingly, in her 1995 essay "The Chicken Tower," Mason laments that the rural life that her father and her ancestors knew is passing. "Their language," she writes, "lingers like relics," and "soon my memories will be loosened from any tangible connection to this land" (479–80). Schomburg points to Mason's reflections of her own life in the modern world and the end of an agrarian way of life. Like many southerners—and like many Americans—Mason admits that we are drawn to those creature comforts that make our lives easier than those of our ancestors. The feast of plenty that may come from the bounty of farming the land also carries with it a burden, as Mason explains in her 1995 essay "The Burden of the Feast." "Granny didn't question her duties," Mason writes, but Mason did. She didn't want to find herself at fifty years old sitting in a hot kitchen hulling beans, and she was thankful for her parents for presenting her with opportunities that led her beyond their home. Despite her move out from the region as a young woman, Mason says, "We always knew where home is" (Schomburg 480).

Mason's *Spence + Lila* (1988) is a powerful example of the conflict between rural lives and the modernization of contemporary life in the South. Spence and Lila Culpepper have farmed their land and raised three children despite difficult times, and now Lila is in a Paducah, Kentucky, hospital, soon to have a mastectomy and surgery on her carotid artery. Characters who represent the heart and soul of America, Lila and Spence and their family deal with the possibility of Lila's death in a high-tech hospital that seems far from their agrarian roots. Their rural world is fast changing, from the subdivisions that have replaced area farms to the factory where Lila and Spence's son works. When Spence looks out over the fields he thinks, "This is it. This is all there is in the world—it contains everything there is to know or possess, yet everywhere people are knocking their brains out trying to find something different, something better . . . Everyone always wants a way out of something like this, but what he has here is the main thing there is" (132).

The "main thing there is" seems far away in *Spence + Lila,* but by the time Mason published her *Clear Springs* in 1999, she seemed to be suggesting new possibilities—especially for herself. When she describes how she "plunged" her hands into the black soil of New England, she writes, "I felt I was touching a rich nourishment that I hadn't had since I was a small child. It had been years since I helped

Mama in the garden. Yet the feel of dirt seems so familiar. This was real. It was true." In response, Mason explains, "I wheeled around and faced home." Place may be the golden thread that always carries us home, according to Welty, but for Mason, digging in the earth reminded her as southerner of the attachment to place and to home. We might not be able to go home again, but Mason seems to have at least tried. Living outside of Lexington, close enough to the airport so that she can make trips beyond the region and nearby the University of Kentucky where she has taught in recent years, Mason says she came back to Kentucky because she believed it was significant for her to return to a community of writers who shared a commitment to their region and to their craft. In wheeling back around and facing home, Mason seems to have like many contemporary southern writers at least worked toward some healing, some reconciliation with the place she once called home but that she fled in her youth.

Such healing mends bridges that don't seem to exist in much of southern literature written before the first Southern Renaissance. For bridges have little part in a world that seems based on boundaries—boundaries that draw lines between the races, between the South and an other (the North, for example), between models of southern womanhood and "other" types of women, between genders, between plantation and farm. The historical South seems to have been built on boundaries that drew sharp distinctions between peoples and places as a means of distinguishing the South from other places, and groups of southerners from other groups of southerners.

Perhaps, though, what has brought down some of those barriers in southern literature of the twentieth century, what has opened opportunities for greater numbers of southern writers, is that the southern story has been reframed. Because of the democratizing of southern literature, that literature has endured and remained distinct. That democratizing is in large part a result of the increasing interest in southern writers of the twentieth century to see the common folk, or the farmer, as the symbol of the South and its potential. The plantation offers none of the possibilities for revival, for closure, and for empowerment. Although some may view the South as a region set in its ways and stuck in the past, it is actually far from it.

The South continues to redefine itself—and in redefining itself it has survived. The South and its literature teach lessons of survival—lessons learned through the devastation of war, the hardships of Reconstruction, the bitter years of the Great Depression, the struggles of the civil rights and women's movements. The South holds on to the possibilities for renewal.

Works Cited

Agar, Herbert, and Allen Tate, eds. *Who Owns America?* Boston: Houghton Mifflin, 1936.

Andrews, William L., ed. *The Literature of the American South.* New York: Norton, 1998.

Arnow, Harriette. *The Dollmaker.* New York: Avon, 1972.

Backman, Melvin. *Faulkner: The Major Years.* Bloomington: Indiana University Press, 1966.

Bell, Bernard W. *The Afro-American Novel and Its Tradition.* Amherst: University of Massachusetts Press, 1987.

Bell, Madison Smartt. "The Booklist Interview: Madison Smartt Bell." By Donna Seaman. *Booklist* 89 (15 April 1993): 1468–69.

———. "An Interview with Madison Smartt Bell." By Mary Louise Weaks. *Southern Review* 30.1 (January 1994): 1–12.

———. *Save Me, Joe Louis.* New York: Harcourt Brace, 1993.

———. *Soldier's Joy: A Novel.* New York: Ticknor and Fields, 1989.

Benson, Brian J., and Mabel Mayle Dillard. *Jean Toomer.* Boston: Twayne, 1980.

Berry, Wendell. *The Unsettling of America: Culture and Agriculture.* San Francisco: Sierra Club, 1977, 1986.

———. "The Work of Local Culture." *What Are People For?* San Francisco: North Point, 1990. 153–169.

Bingham, Emily S., and Thomas A. Underwood, eds. *The Southern Agrarians and the New Deal.* Charlottesville: University Press of Virginia, 2001.

Blotner, Joseph. *Faulkner: A Biography.* New York: Random House, 1974.

Bontemps, Arna. "[Commentary on Jean Toomer and *Cane.*]" *Cane: An Au-*

thoritative Text, Backgrounds, Criticism. Ed. Darwin T. Turner. New York: Norton, 1988. 186–92.

Bradbury, John. *The Fugitives: A Critical Account.* Chapel Hill: University of North Carolina Press, 1958.

Bradford, M. E. "The Passion of Craft." *The History of Southern Literature.* Ed. Louis D. Rubin. Baton Rouge: Louisiana State University Press, 1985. 375–82.

———. "Faulkner and the Jeffersonian Dream." *Mississippi Quarterly* 18.2 (1965): 94–100.

———. "Faulkner's 'Tall Men.'" *South Atlantic Quarterly* 61.1 (1962): 29–39.

———. "Faulkner's 'Tomorrow' and the Plain People." *Studies in Short Fiction* 2.3 (1965): 235–40.

———. "What We Can Know for Certain: Frank Owsley and the Recovery of Southern History." *Sewanee Review* 78 (1970): 664-669.

Brooks, Van Wyck. "On Creating a Usable Past." *Dial* (April 11, 1918): 337–41.

Cash, W. J. *The Mind of the South.* New York: Knopf, 1941.

Cather, Willa. *My Ántonia.* New York: Vintage, 1994.

Chopin, Kate. *The Awakening.* Chicago: Herbert S. Stone, 1899.

Chung, Haeja K. "Harriette Simpson Arnow's Authorial Testimony: Toward a Reading of *The Dollmaker.*" *Critique* 36.3 (1995): 211-24.

Conkin, Paul K. *The Southern Agrarians.* Knoxville: University of Tennessee Press, 1988.

Cook, Sylvia Jenkins. *From Tobacco Road to Route 66: The Southern Poor White in Fiction.* Chapel Hill: University of North Carolina Press, 1976.

Dargan, Olive. *Call Home the Heart: A Novel of the Thirties.* New York: Feminist Press, 1983.

Davidson, Donald. *Lee in the Mountains and Other Poems, including "The Tall Men."* Boston: Houghton Mifflin, 1938.

———. "A Mirror for Artists." *I'll Take My Stand: The South and the Agrarian Tradition.* Baton Rouge: Louisiana State University Press, 1983. 28–60.

———. *The Tennessee.* New York: Rinehart, 1946–48.

Fain, John Tyree, and Thomas Daniel Young, eds. *The Literary Correspondence of Donald Davidson and Allen Tate.* Athens: University of Georgia Press, 1974.

Faulkner, William. *Absalom, Absalom!* New York: Vintage, 1991.

———. *As I Lay Dying.* New York: Vintage, 1990.

———. *A Fable.* New York: Vintage, 1978.

———. *Faulkner at Nagano.* Tokyo: Kenkyusha, 1962.

———. *Light in August.* New York: Vintage, 1991.

————. *The Mansion*. New York: Vintage, 1965.

————. *Requiem for a Nun*. New York: Vintage, 1975.

————. *Sartoris*. New York: Random House, 1956.

————. "Shall Not Perish." *Collected Stories of William Faulkner*. New York: Random House, 1950. 101–115.

————. "The Tall Men." *Collected Stories of William Faulkner*. New York: Random House, 1950. 45–62.

————. "Two Soldiers." *Collected Stories of William Faulkner*. New York: Random House, 1950. 81–100.

————. *The Unvanquished*. New York: Vintage, 1991.

Fitzhugh, George. *Cannibals All!* Ed. C. Vann Woodward. Cambridge: Belknap, 1960.

Foster, Ruel Elton. *Jesse Stuart*. New York: Twayne, 1968.

Fox, John, Jr. *The Little Shepherd of Kingdom Come*. New York: Scribner's, 1903.

Fox-Genovese, Elizabeth, and Eugene D. Genovese. "M. E. Bradford's Historical Vision." *A Defender of Southern Conservatism: M. E. Bradford and His Achievements*. Ed. Clyde N. Wilson. Columbia: University of Missouri Press, 1999. 78–91.

Frank, Waldo. "Foreword." *Cane*. New York: Boni and Liveright, 1923. Rpt. *Cane: An Authoritative Text, Backgrounds, Criticism*. Ed. Darwin T. Turner. New York: Norton, 1988. 138–140.

Gaines, Ernest. *The Autobiography of Miss Jane Pittman*. New York: Dial, 1971.

Glasgow, Ellen. *Barren Ground*. New York: Grosset and Dunlap, 1925.

————. *A Certain Measure*. New York: Harcourt, Brace, 1943.

————. *The Descendent*. New York: Harper, 1905.

————. "The Dynamic Past." *The Reviewer* 1 (1921): 73–80.

————. *In This Our Life*. New York: Harcourt Brace, 1941.

————. *Life and Gabriella*. Garden City, NY: Doubleday, 1916.

————. *Phases of an Inferior Planet*. New York: Harper, 1898.

————. *The Sheltered Life*. Garden City, NY: Doubleday, 1932.

————. *Vein of Iron*. New York: Harcourt, Brace, 1935.

————. *Virginia*. Garden City, NY: Doubleday, 1913.

————. *The Woman Within*. New York: Harcourt Brace, 1954.

Haley, Alex. *Roots*. Garden City, NY: Doubleday, 1976.

Hapke, Laura. *Daughters of the Great Depression: Women, Work, and Fiction in the American 1930s*. Athens: University of Georgia Press, 1995.

Harrison, Elizabeth Jane. *Female Pastoral: Women Writers Re-Visioning the American South*. Knoxville: University of Tennessee Press, 1991.

Helbing, Mark. "Jean Toomer and Waldo Frank: A Creative Friendship." *Jean Toomer: A Critical Evaluation*. Ed. Therman B. O'Daniel. Washington, DC: Howard University Press, 1988. 85–97.

Hentz, Caroline. *The Planter's Northern Bride*. Philadelphia: Hart, 1854.

Hobson, Fred. "Of Canons and Cultural Wars: Southern Literature and Literary Scholarship after Midcentury." *The Future of Southern Letters*. Ed. Jefferson Humphries and John Lowe. New York: Oxford University Press, 1996. 72–86.

Howell, Elmo. "William Faulkner and the Plain People of Yoknapatawpha County." *Journal of Mississippi History* 24.2 (1962): 73–87.

Hurston, Zora Neale. *Their Eyes Were Watching God*. New York: Harper and Row, 1998.

Jefferson, Thomas. *The Life and Selected Writings of Thomas Jefferson*. Franklin Center, PA: Franklin Library, 1982.

Jehlen, Myra. *Class and Character in Faulkner's South*. New York: Columbia University Press, 1976.

Jimerson, Randall C. *The Private Civil War: Popular Thought during the Sectional Conflict*. Baton Rouge: Louisiana State University Press, 1988.

Kelley, William Melvin. *dem*. Garden City, NY: Doubleday, 1967.

King, Grace. "Bayou L'Ombre." *Tales of a Time and Place*. New York: Harper, 1892.

Kreyling, Michael. *Inventing Southern Literature*. Jackson: University Press of Mississippi, 1998.

Levy, Helen Fiddyment. "Coming Home: Glasgow's Last Two Novels." *Ellen Glasgow: New Perspectives*. Ed. Dorothy Scura. Tennessee Studies in Literature, Volume 36. Knoxville: University of Tennessee Press, 1995. 220–234.

Lytle, Andrew. *Bedford Forrest and His Critter Company*. New York: Minton, Blach, 1931.

———. "The Hind Tit." *I'll Take My Stand: The South and the Agrarian Tradition*. Baton Rouge: Louisiana State University Press, 1983. 201–45.

———. *A Name for Evil*. New York: Avon, 1969.

McKay, Nellie. "Jean Toomer in His Time: An Introduction." *Jean Toomer: A Critical Evaluation*. Ed. Therman B. O'Daniel. Washington, DC: Howard University Press, 1988. 3–13.

MacKethan, Lucinda. "Jean Toomer's *Cane*: A Pastoral Problem." *Mississippi Quarterly* 35 (1975): 423–34. Rpt. in *Cane: An Authoritative Text, Backgrounds, Criticism*. Ed. Darwin T. Turner. New York: Norton, 1988. 229–37.

Makowsky, Veronica. *Caroline Gordon: A Biography*. New York: Oxford University Press, 1989.

Malvasi, Mark. "All the Precious Things: M. E. Bradford and the Agrarian Tradition." *A Defender of Southern Conservatism: M. E. Bradford and His Achievements*. Ed. Clyde N. Wilson. Columbia: University of Missouri Press, 1999. 130–42.

Manning, Carol S. "Southern Women Writers and the Beginning of the Renaissance." *The History of Southern Women's Literature*. Ed. Carolyn Perry and Mary Louise Weaks. Baton Rouge: Louisiana State University Press, 2002.

McKay, Nellie. "Jean Toomer in His Time: An Introduction." *Jean Toomer: A Critical Evaluation*. Ed. Therman B. O'Daniel. Washington, DC: Howard University Press, 1988. 3–13.

Mason, Bobbie Ann. *Spence + Lila*. New York: Harper and Row, 1988.

Mellard, James. "The Fiction of Social Commitment." *The History of Southern Literature*. Ed. Louis D. Rubin. Baton Rouge: Louisiana State University Press, 1985. 351–55.

Mitchell, Margaret. *Gone with the Wind*. New York: Avon, 1973.

Nicolaisen, Peter. "William Faulkner's Dialogue with Thomas Jefferson." *Faulkner in America: Faulkner and Yoknapatawpha, 1998*. Ed. Joseph R. Urgo and Ann J. Abadie. Jackson: University Press of Mississippi, 2001. 64–81.

Nixon, Herman Clarence. *Forty Acres and Steel Mules*. Chapel Hill: University of North Carolina Press, 1938.

O'Brien, Michael. *The Idea of the American South, 1920–1941*. Baltimore: Johns Hopkins University Press, 1979.

O'Connor, Flannery. "A Circle in the Fire." *The Complete Stories*. New York: Farrar, Straus, and Giroux, 1972. 175–93.

———. "Good Country People." *The Complete Stories*. New York: Farrar, Straus, Giroux, and 1972. 271–91.

———. "Greenleaf." *The Complete Stories*. New York: Farrar, Straus, and Giroux, 1972. 311–34.

———. *The Habit of Being*. Ed. Sally Fitzgerald. New York: Noonday, 1979.

———. "The Life You Save May Be Your Own." *The Complete Stories*. New York: Farrar, Straus, and Giroux, 1972. 145–56.

———. "Revelation." *The Complete Stories*. New York: Farrar, Straus, and Giroux, 1972. 488–509.

O'Donnell, George Marion. "Looking Down the Cotton Row." *Who Owns America?* Ed. Herbert Agar and Allen Tate. Boston: Houghton Mifflin, 1936. 161–77.

Olmsted, Frederick Law. *A Journey in the Seaboard Slave States*. New York: Dix and Edwards, 1856.

Owsley, Frank. "The Irrepressible Conflict." *I'll Take My Stand*. Baton Rouge: Louisiana State University Press, 1983. 61–91.

———. *Plain Folk of the Old South*. Baton Rouge: Louisiana State University Press, 1949.

Page, Thomas Nelson. *Red Rock: A Chronicle of Reconstruction*. New York: Scribner, 1898.

Ransom, John Crowe. "Bells for John Whiteside's Daughter." *Selected Poems*. New York: Knopf, 1945. 8.

———. "Happy Farmers." *The American Review* 1.5 (1933): 513–35.

———. "Introduction: A Statement of Principles." *I'll Take My Stand: The South and the Agrarian Tradition*. Baton Rouge: Louisiana State University Press, 1983. xxxvii–xlviii.

———. "Janet Waking." *Selected Poems*. New York: Knopf, 1945. 43–44.

———. "Old Mansion." *Selected Poems*. New York: Knopf, 1945. 34–35.

———. "Reconstructed but Unregenerate." *I'll Take My Stand: The South and the Agrarian Tradition*. Baton Rouge: Louisiana State University Press, 1983. 1–27.

Roberts, Elizabeth Madox. *The Time of Man*. Lexington: University Press of Kentucky, 2000.

Rubin, Louis D., Jr. Introduction. *Ellen Glasgow: Centennial Essays*. Ed. Thomas M. Inge. Charlottesville: University Press of Virginia, 1976.

———. Introduction. *I'll Take My Stand: The South and the Agrarian Tradition*. Baton Rouge: Louisiana State University Press, 1977. xi–xxxv.

Rusch, Frederik L., ed. *A Jean Toomer Reader: Selected Unpublished Writings*. New York: Oxford University Press, 1993.

Sanders, Dori. *Clover*. New York: Fawcett Columbine, 1990.

Schomburg, Connie R. "Southern Women Writers in a Changing Landscape." *The History of Southern Women's Literature*. Ed. Carolyn Perry and Mary Louise Weaks. Baton Rouge: Louisiana State University Press, 2002. 478–90.

Scruggs, Charles, and Lee VanDemarr. *Jean Toomer and the Terrors of American History*. Philadelphia: University of Pennsylvania Press, 1998.

Smith, Henry Nash. *Virgin Land: The American West as Symbol and Myth*. New York: Vintage, 1957.

Steinbeck, John. *The Grapes of Wrath*. New York: Penguin, 1976.

Stuart, Jesse. *Beyond Dark Hills: A Personal Story*. New York: Dutton, 1938.

———. *Man with a Bull-Tongued Plow*. New York: Dutton, 1934.

Tate, Allen. "The Fugitive, 1922–1925." *Memoirs and Opinions, 1926–1974*. Chicago: Swallow, 1975. 24–34.

———. *Jefferson Davis: His Rise and Fall*. New York: Minton, Balch, 1929.

———. "A Lost Traveller's Dream." *Memoirs and Opinions, 1926–1974*. Chicago: Swallow, 1975. 3–23.

Tate, Linda. "A Second Southern Renaissance." *The History of Southern Women's Literature*. Ed. Carolyn Perry and Mary Louise Weaks. Baton Rouge: Louisiana State University Press, 2002. 491–97.

Tindall, George Brown. *The Ethnic Southerners*. Baton Rouge: Louisiana State University Press, 1976.

Toomer, Jean. *Cane: An Authoritative Text, Backgrounds, Criticism*. Ed. Darwin T. Turner. New York: Norton, 1988.

———. "Letter to Waldo Frank." n.d., [late 1922 or early 1923]. *Cane: An Authoritative Text, Backgrounds, Criticism*. Ed. Darwin T. Turner. New York: Norton, 1988. 150–51.

———. "The Negro Emergent." *Jean Toomer: Selected Essays and Literary Criticism*. Ed. Robert B. Jones. Knoxville: University of Tennessee Press, 1996. 47–54.

Turner, Darwin T., ed. *Cane: An Authoritative Text, Backgrounds, and Criticism*. New York: Norton, 1988.

Turner, Martha Billips. "The Demise of Mountain Life: Harriette Arnow's Analysis." *Border States: Journal of the Kentucky-Tennessee American Studies Association* 8 (1991): 37–42. *Border States On-line*, http://spider.george towncollege.edu/htallant/border/bs8/turner.htm (10 June 2005).

Underwood, Thomas. *Allen Tate: Orphan of the South*. Princeton: Princeton University Press, 2000.

Urgo, Joseph R. "Where Was that Bird? Thinking *America* through Faulkner." *Faulkner in America: Faulkner and Yoknapatawpha, 1998*. Ed. Joseph R. Urgo and Ann J. Abadie. Jackson: University Press of Mississippi, 2001. 98–115.

———. *Willa Cather and the Myth of American Migration*. Urbana: University of Illinois Press, 1995.

Wagner-Martin, Linda. *Ellen Glasgow: Beyond Convention*. Austin: University of Texas Press, 1982.

Walker, Alice. *The Color Purple*. New York: Washington Square, 1982.

———. "From an Interview." *In Search of Our Mothers' Gardens*. San Diego: Harcourt Brace Jovanovich, 1983. 244–72.

———. "In Search of Our Mothers' Gardens." *In Search of Our Mothers' Gardens*. San Diego: Harcourt Brace Jovanovich, 1983. 231–43.

Walker, Margaret. *Jubilee*. Boston: Houghton, Mifflin, 1966.

Warren, Robert Penn. *Brother to Dragons*. New York: Random House, 1979.

———. "Talk with Robert Penn Warren." By Benjamin DeMott. *Talking with Robert Penn Warren.* Ed. Floyd C. Watkins, John T. Hiers, and Mary Louise Weaks. Athens: University of Georgia Press, 1990. 227–32.

Watson, Ritchie Devon, Jr. *Yeoman versus Cavalier: The Old Southwest's Fictional Road to Rebellion.* Baton Rouge: Louisiana State University Press, 1993.

Welty, Eudora. *Delta Wedding.* New York: Harcourt, Brace, 1946.

Whites, LeeAnn. *The Civil War as a Crisis in Gender: Augusta, Georgia, 1860–1890.* Athens: University of Georgia Press, 1995.

Wilson, Charles Regan, and William Ferris, eds. *The Encyclopedia of Southern Culture.* Chapel Hill, NC: University of North Carolina Press, 1989.

Wintz, Cary D. *Black Culture and the Harlem Renaissance.* Houston: Rice University Press, 1988.

Woodward, C. Vann. *Origins of the New South, 1877–1913.* Baton Rouge: Louisiana State University Press, 1951.

Young, Thomas Daniel. *Waking Their Neighbors Up: The Nashville Agrarians Rediscovered.* Athens: University of Georgia Press, 1982.

Young, Thomas Daniel, and George Core, eds. *Selected Letters of John Crowe Ransom.* Baton Rouge: Louisiana State University Press, 1985.

Index

Agrarians, 53; number of publications by, 51; and Stuart, 81, 82, 83, 86, 90, 95; at Vanderbilt University, 38, 82; on yeomanry, 40, 44–46

—works: "A Mirror for Artists," 46–47; *The Old War*, 45; *The Tall Men*, 44–46; *The Tennessee*, 46

Davis, Jefferson, 42–44

Deep South versus Upper South, 41–47

Delta Wedding (Welty), 157–59

Dem (Kelley), 121

Democracy and Poetry (Warren), 55

Descendent, The (Glasgow), 17

Distributist movement, 40, 51, 52

Dollmaker, The (Arnow), 6, 139, 147–51, 156

Douglass, Frederick, 138

Eliot, T. S., 67

Ellison, Ralph, 76, 139

"Everyday Use" (Walker), 149

Fable, A (Faulkner), 120

Farmers. *See* Pioneers; Yeomanry

Faulkner, Charles J., 10

Faulkner, William: African Americans in works by, 118, 127; Bradford's interpretation of, 14, 120–23, 126–28, 132–35; farm of, 117; Genovese and Fox-Genovese on, 14, 128; Grier family in, 123, 128, 132–33, 134; Howell's interpretation of, 120–21, 122, 123, 126–28; Jefferson, Miss., in works by, 117–18; Jehlen's interpretation of, 118–19; literary criticism of generally, 116; and map of Yoknapatawpha County, 118, 127; McCallum family in, 122, 123, 124–26, 128–32, 133; McCaslin brothers in, 122–23, 133–34; Nicolaisen's interpretation of, 117–20; Nobel Prize acceptance speech by, 131,

132; physical appearance of, 117; and planter myth, 115; planters in works by, 117–19; Sartoris family in, 123–25; Snopes family in, 146; tension between yeoman and planter traditions in, 117–18; Urgo on, 137; yeomanry in works by, 14, 117–35

—works: *Absalom, Absalom!*, 114; *As I Lay Dying*, 123; *A Fable*, 120; *Light in August*, 123; *The Mansion*, 123; "The Old Man," 123; "Race at Morning," 123; *Requiem for a Nun*, 117–18; *Sartoris*, 123–26; "Shall Not Perish," 123, 128, 132–33; "The Tall Men," 120, 123, 128–33; "Tomorrow," 123; "Two Soldiers," 123, 128, 132; *The Unvanquished*, 133–34

Female characters. *See* Women characters

Fitzhugh, George, 10

Fletcher, John Gould, 40, 51

Forrest, Mariam, 43

Forrest, Nathan Bedford, 42–43

Forty Acres and Steel Mules (Nixon), 52

"Foundation of Democracy, The" (Owsley), 53

Fox, John, Jr., 158

Fox-Genovese, Elizabeth, 14, 128

Frank, Waldo, 59, 66, 69–70, 77, 78

Frost, Robert, 91

Fugitive, The 38, 44, 45

Fugitives, 38, 41, 44, 45

Gaines, Ernest, 121

Gastonia mill strike, 105–6

Genovese, Eugene D., 14, 128

Glasgow, Ellen: on industrialization, 29, 33; influence of, on other writers, 36; on marriage, 17–18, 33–35; parents of, 20–21; on pioneers, 28–36; on progress for the South, 24; on survival and

Sheltered Life, The (Glasgow), 18
Sherman, William T., 42
Slavery: Bradford on, 127, 128; C. J.
    Faulkner on abolition of, 10; Geno-
    vese and Fox-Genovese on, 128;
    Jefferson as slave owner, 9; Owsley
    on, 50; and planter ideal, 10, 11, 13;
    Toomer on, 59; Warren on, 55. *See also*
    Planter myth
"Small Farm Secures the State, The"
    (Lytle), 53
Small farmers. *See* Yeomanry
Smith, Henry Nash, 11
Smith, Lee, 80
Soldier's Joy (Bell), 160–61, 162
Southern belle, 16, 18, 102–3, 114
Southern conservatism, 122, 127, 128
Southern Literary Renaissance: begin-
    ning of, 2, 38; and creation of "usable
    past" for United States, 14–15; and
    dismantling façades, 2; façade-build-
    ing during, 2; and figure of common
    man and woman, 4–7, 157; influence
    of, on later writers, 157–73; and mi-
    gration of southerners, 138, 155–56;
    and Toomer, 6, 61, 77–78; and women
    writers, 2. *See also* Agrarians; *and spe-
    cific authors*
Southern literary studies, 115–16. *See
    also specific critics*
Spence + Lila (Mason), 171
Steinbeck, John, 138, 139–40, 145,
    151–52, 154–55
Still, James, 80
Stuart, Jesse: and Agrarians, 81; ances-
    tors of, 87; on beauty of Appalachian
    Mountains, 92; and Davidson, 81,
    82, 83, 86, 90, 95; on death, 92–93;
    education of, 81–82, 83, 86, 88, 93; as
    farmer, 85–86; fiction by, 80, 88–89;
    on God, 90; Guggenheim fellowship

for, 84; hillman persona of, 86–87;
    independence of, as writer, 79, 88–89;
    and mountain music, 93; and pastoral
    tradition, 93; poetic voice of, 79, 84–
    86, 92; publishing history and awards
    of, 80–81; and southern Appalachian
    Mountains, 5; on Southern Appa-
    lachian region as American, 94–95;
    struggle of, over Kentucky home, 84;
    as teacher in mountain communities,
    80–81; themes of poetry by, 82–83; on
    ties to and primacy of the land, 87–91;
    on tragedy in Appalachian Moun-
    tains, 91–92
—works: *Beyond Dark Hills*, 81–86, 88–
    93; *Man with a Bull-Tongue Plow*, 79,
    80, 82–95; *Taps for Private Tussie*, 80;
    The Thread That Runs So True, 80–81;
    "The Trail," 83–84
Suffrage for women, 96, 97
Swallow Barn (Kennedy), 10
Sydnor, Charles S., 11

Tall Men, The (Davidson), 44–46
"Tall Men, The" (Faulkner), 120, 123, 128–33
Taps for Private Tussie (Stuart), 80
Tate, Allen: and agrarian experiment at
    Benfolly, 53–54; as Agrarian gener-
    ally, 37, 38, 116; biography of, 53;
    birthplace of, 42; on Civil War, 42; on
    cotton industry, 42; and Distributist
    movement, 40, 51; migration by, 155;
    mother of, 41–42; on national versus
    southern goals of Agrarians, 53; as
    New Critic, 116; on South and its his-
    tory, 56; on Upper South versus Deep
    South, 42, 43–44; at Vanderbilt Uni-
    versity, 38; on yeomanry, 40
—works: *Ancestors of Exile*, 41–42;
    Jefferson Davis, 42, 43–44; "A Lost
    Traveler's Dream," 41, 42